Ruth

Ruth

Taking Refuge Under God's Wings

BOB CANODE

WIPF & STOCK · Eugene, Oregon

RUTH
Taking Refuge Under God's Wings

Copyright © 2026 Bob Canode. All rights reserved. Except for brief quotations in critical publications or reviews, no part of this book may be reproduced in any manner without prior written permission from the publisher. Write: Permissions, Wipf and Stock Publishers, 199 W. 8th Ave., Suite 3, Eugene, OR 97401.

Wipf & Stock
An Imprint of Wipf and Stock Publishers
199 W. 8th Ave., Suite 3
Eugene, OR 97401

www.wipfandstock.com

PAPERBACK ISBN: 979-8-3852-6527-5
HARDCOVER ISBN: 979-8-3852-6528-2
EBOOK ISBN: 979-8-3852-6529-9

VERSION NUMBER 010226

Scripture quotations are taken from the ESV® Bible (The Holy Bible, English Standard Version®), © 2001 by Crossway, a publishing ministry of Good News Publishers. ESV Text Edition: 2025. The ESV text may not be quoted in any publication made available to the public by a Creative Commons license. The ESV may not be translated in whole or in part into any other language. Used by permission. All rights reserved.

To my wife, Adelinda

Contents

Acknowledgments | ix
Introduction | xi

Part I: Emptiness and Loyalty

Chapter 1: Leaving Home | 3
   Ruth 1:1–5

Chapter 2: Returning Home | 11
   Ruth 1:6–9

Chapter 3: A Daughter Clings | 17
   Ruth 1:10–14

Chapter 4: A Daughter Confesses | 23
   Ruth 1:15–18

Chapter 5: Arriving Home | 30
   Ruth 1:19–22

Part II: Ruth and Boaz

Chapter 1: An Introduction | 39
   Ruth 2:1–7

Chapter 2: Conversation | 47
   Ruth 2:8–13

Chapter 3: Dining Together | 53
   Ruth 2:14–16

Chapter 4: Telling Naomi | 59
   Ruth 2:17–23

Part III: The Threshing Floor

Chapter 1: Initiation of the Plan | 67
   Ruth 3:1–5

Chapter 2: Execution of the Plan | 73
   Ruth 3:6–9
Chapter 3: Response | 79
   Ruth 3:10–13
Chapter 4: Return | 85
   Ruth 3:14–18

Part IV: Redemption and Royalty

Chapter 1: A Name Removed | 93
   Ruth 4:1–6
Chapter 2: A Name Redeemed | 99
   Ruth 4:7–10
Chapter 3: A Name Renowned | 103
   Ruth 4:11–12
Chapter 4: Arrival of a Son | 107
   Ruth 4:13
Chapter 5: Song of the Son | 111
   Ruth 4:14–15
Chapter 6: Servant | 118
   Ruth 4:16–17
Chapter 7: Breach | 124
   Ruth 4:18–22

Conclusion | 131

Bibliography | 133

Acknowledgments

I GIVE THE HIGHEST thanks to my Redeemer, my gō'ēl, Jesus Christ. Like that done to Ruth and Naomi, he brought me out of a land of death and filled me with his abundant life.

In union with Christ, I accomplish nothing in isolation. This book has one author but it is the product of many. For the dear laborers at Wipf and Stock, I offer my utmost gratitude. I am thankful for their courage to embrace this material and for their investment in me as I enter the publishing world.

I would like to thank every member of Providence Presbyterian Church. I was inspired to preach through Ruth on two separate occasions to encourage the saints at our local church. It is because of them that this work has a genesis. Their unwavering support of my ministry through the years has kept me moving forward and for this I am eternally grateful.

Many thanks go to the elders who serve with me on our local session. Their patience with me is undeserved. I would not be able to pursue a work like this without their friendship and labor. I am thankful for the time off for study leave to focus on this project. Likewise, our deacons inspire me to serve the broader church like they faithfully serve our congregation.

It would be inappropriate not to specify one church member whose help was invaluable. A thousand thanks go to Tiffany Price. Her labors in editing provided clarity and sharpness to my rough drafts. If anyone should regard this book as well-written, she deserves much of the credit.

I give thanks to my children. The light of your faces illuminates my days. As I worked on this project, the sights and sounds of your lives and your growth in grace gave me strength to persevere. May this book grant you but a portion of the joy you bring to me each day.

To my wife, Adelinda, thank you for encouraging me and never letting me settle for less than what God has called me to be and to do. By faith, you followed me into this life of gospel ministry. Not one word written here

Acknowledgments

would see the light of day without you. This book is dedicated to you. You are my Ruth.

Introduction

I HAVE FOUND THAT whether I am engaged in preaching, Sunday school teaching, or in private reading in the book of Ruth, it always delivers a spiritual punch. It is one of the smaller books in the Old Testament and much, much smaller than the two books that serve as Ruth's bookends in a modern English translation: Judges and 1 Samuel.[1] Nestled in between these two books, and all but buried in the midst of other textual giants such as Genesis, Exodus, Deuteronomy, Joshua, 2 Samuel, Kings, and Chronicles, Ruth seems to be out of place. A cursory examination of the internal characteristics of this book also may support such an opinion. There are no great battles fought in Ruth. Angels do not come down from heaven. God does not speak through direct revelation nor does he speak through the thunderous warnings of a prophet or through ecstatic visions. No divine miracles are reported. Kings are not exalted to power over vast kingdoms nor are they ignominiously taken down in a blaze of glory. There are no accounts of political intrigue or betrayal. And yet, the terseness and simplicity of Ruth have a power all their own. Like with an atom bomb or dynamite, a surface level assessment might leave one confused as to its potential power. But the confusion would quickly vanish upon detonation. The power would be *seen* and *felt*. It is the goal of this work that we might begin to see and feel this book's potential.

This is partly done by considering *all* that we are given in God's word, not just one book. The biblical accounts of the parting of the Red Sea, the stoppage of the sun during the conquest of Canaan, Samson's great strength, David's victory over Goliath and his rise to power as king of Israel, Daniel in the lion's den, and Elijah raising the dead and his spiritual contest against the prophets of Baal, among others, all direct us to the mercy and

---

1. Longman and Dillard, *Introduction to the Old Testament*, 144. Ruth is located toward the end of the traditional Hebrew Bible, after Proverbs and before the Song of Solomon.

Introduction

power of the one true and living God in heaven who reveals his glory and infinite might through events in history such as this. The miracles of Jesus Christ lead us in the same direction. For Jesus is our Emmanuel, "God with us." The New Testament gives us a record of the miracles performed by Christ's apostles. These men were uniquely endowed by the Holy Spirit to do miracles in the name of Christ. In each case, the apostles taught and preached that the power revealed in the miracles came from Jesus, the Son of God made flesh. All of this, as it is given to us in Holy Scripture, is meant to convey to man that we are in need of *supernatural* intervention. Salvation for sinful man *must* come from above or it does not come at all. This is a necessary component of gospel teaching.

At the same time, while we need to know and remember that the all-powerful God of heaven and earth has worked gloriously and supernaturally in history to bring about the salvation of his people, we also need to understand how these accounts of God's mighty acts of redemption should shape our daily lives. For most Christian families, the days we are given are beset, in varying degrees, by the ordinary aspects of life found in Ruth: family relationships, business ventures, property concerns, economic downturns, economic upturns, the joys of marriage, the difficulties of marriage, the ups and downs of widowhood, raising children, holding grandchildren, dating, being single, grief over death, feelings of loneliness and bitterness, disappointments, unexpected joy, planning weddings, attending weddings, drinking wine, eating food, working daily at our jobs or at home, waiting and searching for a husband or wife, moving to a different location, and the praise of God in the gathered worship of God's people. While this list is not exhaustive, it does touch upon what Christians ordinarily face in this life and the things with which we are most concerned.

As we will see in the following pages, this was the case as well for many Israelite families, holding on to the promises of a coming Messiah, and living, as we are told in the very first line of this book, "in the days when the judges ruled" (Ruth 1:1). While other books of the Bible that are filled with extraordinary events do give us lessons for our daily lives, Ruth seems to be focused *only* on the ordinary. Thus, if we have eyes to see and ears to hear, we can find a deep connection with the story recounted here. We may also identify, at certain points, with its characters, who, for the most part, are portrayed as *less than* extraordinary, even as a sovereign God directs their lives in such a way as to bring about the arrival of an extraordinary Savior, Jesus Christ. May the Lord be pleased to use what is written here to lead

INTRODUCTION

you to *him*. For it is the power of his gospel that is enclosed within this small physical frame—the book of Ruth.

Part I: Emptiness and Loyalty

Chapter 1: Leaving Home

RUTH 1:1–5

In the days when the judges ruled there was a famine in the land, and a man of Bethlehem in Judah went to sojourn in the country of Moab, he and his wife and his two sons. The name of the man was Elimelech and the name of his wife Naomi, and the names of his two sons were Mahlon and Chilion. They were Ephrathites from Bethlehem in Judah. They went into the country of Moab and remained there. But Elimelech, the husband of Naomi, died, and she was left with her two sons. These took Moabite wives; the name of the one was Orpah and the name of the other Ruth. They lived there about ten years, and both Mahlon and Chilion died, so that the woman was left without her two sons and her husband.

THE TITLE OF THE book is Ruth and for good reason. Ruth certainly is a prominent figure in the story. We find ourselves enraptured by the story of a young widow who leaves her native land to become a foreigner in another, unsure of what kind of life awaits her there. Ruth is mentioned in Matthew's genealogy of Christ at the beginning of his Gospel. This is significant, considering she is one of only four women mentioned there, among a long list of the names of fathers. As much as Ruth is central to the story recounted in the book of her namesake, it could be argued that the book is really about Boaz. By the time we get to the last chapter of the book we realize that this is where we were headed all along—to *him*. He is not mentioned in the first chapter, but he is in the background, in Judah, ready to be introduced into

Part I: Emptiness and Loyalty

Ruth and Naomi's life at the proper time. This introduction will happen because of God's wise and holy providence of course. In chapter 1, though, we would do well to remember that it is *to Boaz* that Ruth and Naomi's path is directed. And so, it would not be incorrect to say that the book of Ruth is about Boaz. We could go further and say that the book of Ruth is about Boaz and how Boaz is a type of Christ. But for now, we may simply think about Boaz until his introduction in the next chapter. With this in mind, we could go further still and say that the book of Ruth is about Boaz *and* Ruth. The book is about Boaz and his relation to Ruth, and Ruth and her relation to Boaz. It is about this particular relationship and how their life together fits in with God's plan for his people.

So, we are heading toward Boaz in the story. But first, we must consider the way in which the story begins. Ruth begins with much emptiness. In the very first verse we are given the time frame of this couple's story: "In the days when the judges ruled" (v. 1). This was the time in Israel's history when there was no king. The leadership position was empty. If we consider Israel's history up until this point, we would remember that under Joshua's leadership, Israel, as a people, had reached a kind of peak in terms of their obedience to God's word and the blessings they received from him as a result of that obedience. Under Joshua's leadership (and the leadership of Caleb), Israel took possession of Canaan. The sweeping victory of the Israelites over the pagan forces in Canaan, as recorded in the book of Joshua, was swift and comprehensive. It was a testament to the kind of success God's people could have under strong, faithful leadership, such as was found in Joshua and Caleb. But time rolled on and both Joshua, Caleb, and all that generation died. And we are told in Scripture, "there arose another generation after them who did not know the LORD or the work he had done for Israel" (Judg 2:10). Thus, the people of God fell into sin. Without strong leadership, the people of God quickly spiraled into a moral and spiritual decline. In response to their disobedience, God allowed the surrounding pagan nations to continually harass the Israelites. As this penetrating military pressure from the surrounding gentile nations was felt, the Israelites would cry out to God for deliverance. And in response to their cries, God mercifully gave them judges to rule for a time, and it was through their leadership that God gave his people salvation from their enemies. This is the pattern displayed in the book of Judges, and "in the days when the judges ruled." God's people would sin. God would send a foreign nation to oppress them for their disobedience. The people of God, overwhelmed by the oppression,

Chapter 1: Leaving Home

would then cry out to God for deliverance. In answer to those prayers, the LORD would raise up a judge-deliverer to save them.

During this time period God's people did enjoy, for certain amounts of time, peace and deliverance under the rule of the judges. But once the judge passed from the scene, what followed was further spiritual waywardness and sin among the people. And so, the pattern above was repeated. In addition to this, the judges themselves lacked the God-centered confidence and thoroughgoing integrity of men like Joshua and Caleb. So there was a leadership vacuum in the time of Ruth. And without strong leadership, the people fell into sin and darkness over and over again. The last line of the book of Judges sums up the spiritual environment in Israel when Ruth and Naomi meet: "In those days there was no king in Israel. Everyone did what was right in their own eyes" (Judg 21:25). God's people were spiritually empty. The leadership position was empty. God's promises about the future glory of Israel seemed empty. And now, at the beginning of this story, we read that the physical land is struck with emptiness as well: "In the days when the judges ruled there was a famine in the land" (Ruth 1:1).

The writer doesn't tell us precisely *why* there was a famine. However, God had already warned his people that he would curse the fruit of the ground if they rebelled against him. These are the words of God, through Moses, to his people prior to entering the promised land: "But if you will not obey the voice of the LORD your God or be careful to do all his commandments and his statutes that I command you today, then all these curses shall come upon you.... The heavens over your head shall be bronze, and the earth under you shall be iron. The LORD will make the rain of your land powder" (Deut 28:15, 23–24). Therefore, during this time of the rule of judges when everyone in Israel "did what was right in their own eyes," it is likely that this famine was part of a curse from God to discipline his people for their sin.[1] In the days that they took possession of this fruitful land and began to prosper in it, the Israelites were not to rebel against God and forget him. The threatened curses for this kind of behavior were dire.

Without a proper food supply in Israel, what were the families living here supposed to do? In particular, what was Elimelech to do with his family, this man of Bethlehem in Judah?[2] God gave commandments to his people in regard to this potential scenario, as well. Once again, these are the

---

1. Block, *Judges, Ruth*, 624; Ferguson, *Faithful God*, 22–23.

2. Bethlehem means "house of bread." Hubbard comments, "How ironic that the 'house of bread' failed to feed this family!" *Book of Ruth*, 85.

Part I: Emptiness and Loyalty

words of God through Moses before the Israelite families had ever set their feet on Canaanite soil: "When the Lord your God brings you into the land that you are entering to take possession of it, and clears away many nations before you, . . . you shall make no covenant with them. . . . You shall not intermarry with them, giving your daughters to their sons or taking their daughters for your sons, for they would turn away your sons from following me, to serve other gods" (Deut 7:1–4).

Covenanting with the foreign nations surrounding Judah and the rest of Israel was always a temptation. If food was scarce in the land, then maybe God's people should look to *other* lands and *other* people who serve *other* gods to find food. But God had given his word in regard to this as well:

> And when all these things come upon you, the blessing and the curse, which I have set before you, and you call them to mind among all the nations where the Lord your God has driven you, and return to the Lord your God, you and your children and obey his voice in all that I command you today, with all your heart and with all your soul, then the Lord your God will restore your fortunes and have mercy on you. (Deut 30:1–3)

The Israelites were clearly told not to covenant with the pagan nations surrounding them. The writer of Ruth doesn't tell us Elimelech's motives or desires in moving his family to Moab during this famine that struck the land of Judah. But if it was true that God struck Bethlehem with a famine because of sin then the remedy would not have been to move, but to *repent*. Turn from sin and the curse for sin would be removed. In light of God's commandments, Elimelech, as a leader of this family, deciding to move to Moab to find refuge from the famine in Judah was not a wise choice, and the results of this move proved the same. An Israelite in the Old Testament, listening to this story, would have most likely paused already at the point when the sojourn to Moab was mentioned: "And a man of Bethlehem in Judah went to sojourn in the country of Moab, he and his wife and his two sons" (Ruth 1:1). He might have been thinking to himself, "This may not turn out so well for them."

The writer specifically names our characters here: "The name of the man was Elimelech and the name of his wife Naomi and the names of his two sons were Mahlon and Chilion. They were Ephrathites from Bethlehem in Judah. They went into the country of Moab and remained there" (v. 2). Throughout the book, there are repeated references to family members: a mother, her sons, and her daughters-in-law. Naomi becomes the

Chapter 1: Leaving Home

mother-in-law to Ruth, a Moabite woman. The book ends with a family tree or genealogy. Prior to the genealogy, in the last scene of the story, Naomi is holding her new grandson, born to Boaz and Ruth. This grandson, Obed, as we learn in the family tree, will himself have a grandson, David, the king of Israel. Why is the emphasis on family members significant? First, the book of Ruth answers what may have been a serious question in the hearts of the Israelites at this time. There was no established leader or king, and everyone did what was right in their own eyes. So, there was chaos within the families of Judah and there was chaos from without. There was famine in the land and harassment from the surrounding gentile nations. A member of God's covenant people might have been asking himself, "What is God doing?" The answer is found here: the book of Ruth. *This* is what God was doing. While his people, on the whole, remained unfaithful, God remained faithful. He was preparing the way for a king to be born to Israel. It is not an accident that much of this story takes place in Bethlehem, the very city in which Jesus was born (Mic 5:2; Matt 2:6).

The second aspect we should consider, as we think about the way in which Ruth contains an emphasis on family members, is that God was doing this great work, preparing the way for a king, precisely *through* families. To put it in perspective, God was advancing his plan for the salvation of countless souls from all over the world to a thousand generations, *through* the intimate workings of this small, lowly Jewish family: Elimelech, Naomi, Mahlon, and Chilion. As Christians, we would do well to appreciate the fact that God is *still* doing this. He is still advancing his plan of salvation for countless souls through *families*. The way in which a husband and wife love one another matters to God. The way in which parents lead their children matters to God. How children serve their siblings and parents matters to God. To be sure, there is only one family tree of David and of Christ. The families involved in the program of redemptive history leading up to Christ experienced events that are unrepeatable. What continues, however, is the ministry of the gospel in the church. The Bible is explicit in regard to the significance of family members and their obedience to the gospel:

> Husbands, love your wives, as Christ loved the church and gave himself up for her. (Eph 5:25)

> Wives, be subject to your own husbands, so that even if some do not obey the word, they may be won without a word by the conduct of their wives. (1 Pet 3:1)

Part I: Emptiness and Loyalty

> Children, obey your parents in the Lord, for this is right. (Eph 6:1)

> Hear, my son, your father's instruction, and forsake not your mother's teaching. (Prov 1:8)

The love that family members have for one another in the church is evidence to the world of our love for Christ and the transformative power of the gospel. In accordance with God's will, the children we are raising today will serve, tomorrow, as the next generation of God's people in a world full of misery and temptation. In that day, God will continue to use them, as members of the body of Christ, to build up the saints and draw the elect to the hearing of the gospel. Therefore, we can state again something of what we learn in Ruth—what we do in our families matters to God.

By the end of chapter 1, Naomi looked at family life differently. She felt insignificant. In her eyes, her life and the life of her family did not matter to God. In fact, he would take away three prominent members in her family in death (Ruth 1:3–5). After this, she wanted to be called Mara, which means "bitter," instead of Naomi ("pleasant") because God had dealt bitterly with her (v. 20). She didn't have much hope for her future. Nevertheless, her desires, her fears, her actions and words, they all mattered to God. They have been recorded in this book for generation after generation to consider. It is the same for us today. The activities, behaviors, and words that happen within our families may seem trivial, insignificant. But the book of Ruth reminds us that in God's eyes they are far from insignificant. For it is within the context of families where the gospel is lived out. Shortly, we will see the commitment and love shared between a mother and her daughter-in-law and how God used this to bless this family, and indeed the whole world. We must persevere in our faithfulness at home with our families. This matters to God. He knows our names, the names of our children and grandchildren. He knows all of our fears and desires and he loves us. We live in a dark world where many people do whatever is right in their own eyes. But families committed to Christ and his church do not. We share the same world, but not the same desires. We are called to holiness in the midst of a perverse generation. And we are called to trust that the Lord will advance his kingdom in us and through us to the praise of his glory, regardless of how small and insignificant we may feel.

Verse 2 tells us that the whole family remained in Moab during the famine: "They went into the country of Moab and remained there." In verses three and five we see that the men in this family remain in Moab in more

Chapter 1: Leaving Home

ways than one: "But Elimelech, the husband of Naomi died . . . and both Mahlon and Chilion died" (vv. 3–5). Elimelech decided to move his family to Moab in order to escape death. Instead, he walks right into it. Elimelech dies. The land was emptied of food, and now Naomi has been emptied of her husband. Thus, the male leadership role in this family falls upon the sons, who are mentioned at the end of verse 3: "And she was left with her two sons." And what do the sons choose to do? "These took Moabite wives" (v. 4). Now, we can pause here again. An Israelite listening to this story would most likely be very concerned. God strictly forbade Israelite families from giving their daughters to Canaanite men in marriage and from Israelite sons taking Canaanite women to be their wives. This has already been seen in the passage from Deuteronomy listed above: "You shall not intermarry with them" (Deut 7:3). The result that would come about by ignoring this prohibition would be that the anger of the LORD would be kindled against them and he would destroy them quickly (Deut 7:4). And yet, this is exactly what these two sons actually do: "These took Moabite wives." Naomi now has two daughters-in-law, Orpah and Ruth. The Israelite listener might say to himself once again, "This may not turn out well for them."

Indeed, it doesn't. The writer doesn't tell us explicitly that the deaths of Naomi's sons were a judgment from God for taking Canaanite wives. However, based on Old Testament law, this is certainly a possibility, and a strong possibility at that. Nevertheless, God did foreordain that these three men would die in Moab: "Mahlon and Chilion died" (Ruth 1:5). Naomi confirms in verse 20 that it was because of the LORD, not blind chance, that all of this has taken place: "The Almighty has dealt very bitterly with me." In the short span of about ten years (v. 4) Naomi has lost nearly everything important to her. The verdict on her plight at this point is driven home for the reader in the last part of verse 5: "So that the woman was left without her two sons and her husband." She had been made empty.[3] Naomi is emptied, and it is God who has done this. Naomi again confirms this fact in verse 21: "I went away full and the LORD brought me back empty."

Thus, we are introduced to two of the main characters in this story, Naomi and Ruth. But in this section the focus is on Naomi. At this point it seems as though *death* is the victor in Naomi's life and in the land of Judah as well. Naomi and the land are related here. The fruit of the land died in the famine. Naomi's husband and her two sons died in Moab. Her situation seemed very bleak. As Christians, sometimes our lives look this way to us.

---

3. Hubbard, *Book of Ruth*, 96–97.

Part I: Emptiness and Loyalty

Maybe this is so because of death or because of some other life changing event. This is what the circumstances looked like for the people of God when Jesus died. The supposed Messiah, the king of Israel, was bound and crucified on a Roman cross. His body was buried. Death and emptiness seemed to be victorious that day. The apostle Paul says that Christ coming to earth and dying a sinner's death was the way in which Jesus *emptied* himself (Phil 2:5–8). But Jesus, though under the sentence of death for a time, was on his way to rising from the dead and entering into *permanent* resurrection life, not only for himself but for all believers, from every generation.

As we go through this book, we will see how God does this over and over again in the lives of his people. He brings life *through death*.[4] In the very next verse, after the report of Naomi's emptiness in verse 5, we already see a hint of God doing this in the land of Judah. We are told here that Naomi and her two daughters-in-law begin a return trip back to the land of Judah because Naomi had heard that "the LORD had visited his people and given them food" (Ruth 1:6). He filled the ground with fruit again and he would fill Naomi too. She just did not know this yet.

For us as Christians, we may feel as though God has brought us back empty. And perhaps he has. We go through times when it feels as if death, sin, division, and emptiness are the victors in our lives. But this book reminds us they are not. The resurrection of Christ tells us they are not. We are called to be patient, to remain steadfast and trust in the LORD. He brings life through death. Though he empties us, he will fill us again.

---

4. Ferguson, *Faithful God*, 38–39.

Chapter 2: Returning Home

RUTH 1:6–9

Then she arose with her daughters-in-law to return from the country of Moab, for she had heard in the fields of Moab that the Lord had visited his people and given them food. So she set out from the place where she was with her two daughters-in-law, and they went on the way to return to the land of Judah. But Naomi said to her two daughters-in-law, "Go, return each of you to her mother's house. May the Lord deal kindly with you, as you have dealt with the dead and with me. The Lord grant that you may find rest, each of you in the house of her husband!" Then she kissed them, and they lifted up their voices and wept.

ALMOST AS SOON AS we hear about Naomi's plight, we hear about God's goodness to her in the midst of her suffering. The next several verses reveal interchanges between Naomi and her two Moabite daughters-in-law, Ruth and Orpah. After these verbal exchanges between the three women, in the end, it is Naomi and Ruth who travel together back to Judah. We must remember that up until this point, the setting of the story is still Moab.[1] But Naomi and Ruth would end up returning to Bethlehem in Judah. In this chapter we will consider the first discussion.

In verses 6–9, the only sound that comes from the two Moabite women is weeping: "They lifted up their voices and wept" (v. 9). So, the focus in

---

1. Hubbard, *Book of Ruth*, 102.

Part I: Emptiness and Loyalty

these verses is on Naomi. We have said that in this section we are already beginning to see God's abundant mercy to her. In the previous section, the text also focuses on Naomi: "But Elimelech, the husband of Naomi, died, and she was left with her two sons ... and both Mahlon and Chilion died, so that the woman was left without her two sons and her husband" (vv. 3–5). The emphasis is on "the woman," Naomi, who has been bereft of husbands and sons. But then all of a sudden, Naomi is on the move: "Then she arose with her daughters-in-law to return from the country of Moab" (v. 6). Thus, the setting begins to shift from Moab. This is significant because the story began with a Jewish family moving to Moab in search of food and life—a safe refuge from famine. What did Moab prove to be for them? It was a land of death. To Naomi, Moab was a land of graves, three of them to be exact. Elimelech and Naomi had hoped their family would be *filled* in Moab. Instead, they were *emptied*. The three men in this family succumbed to death in Moab. Naomi's hope for a prosperous future and the continuation of her husband's family line was all but extinguished in Moab. This is what sin and death do. The death of a loved one, sins of others and sins of our own, can leave us thinking that there is no hope for our future. Maybe it is *our own* death, the prospect of death, that has us thinking negatively about our future and possibly even about God's goodness. This is the kind of inner turmoil Naomi was contending with. She knew that God was sovereign. But was he *good*? Could Naomi trust that God would be good to her when, as she put it, the Lord had dealt so bitterly with her (v. 13)?

One of the good things that God had already done in all of this, which Naomi initially did not appreciate, is found in the two other women, Ruth and Orpah. Even though God had taken away three men, he *added* two women to this family.[2] Naomi has two daughters-in-law, when before she had none. One of these women, Ruth, will provide Naomi with her first grandchild. Sometimes, when we are suffering or when death is knocking at our door, we have blinders on to the very good gifts that God has given us—gifts of mercy, which are right before our eyes. During times like this, we can tend to only focus on what we *don't* have. Such was Naomi's vision at this time. We will look at this more closely in the following chapters, but for now, Naomi and her two daughters-in-law are travelling *away* from Moab and, therefore, *away* from what proved to be, for this family, a land of death.

---

2. Hubbard writes, "She is not totally destitute; against three losses (Elimelech, Mahlon, Chilion) she has at least two gains (Orpah, Ruth); and now she can go home." *Book of Ruth*, 100–101.

Chapter 2: Returning Home

The text refers to the beginning of their travels as a return: "Then she arose with her daughters-in-law to return from the country of Moab" (v. 6). The word translated here as "return," *shub*, and also translated as "turn back" or "gone back" elsewhere, relays a prominent theme in this chapter.[3] A form of this word is used nine times in chapter 1, e.g., "They went on the way to return to the land of Judah" (v. 7); "But Naomi said, return each of you" (v. 8); "No, we will return with you to your people" (v. 10). There are two paths in this story. One path leads to Moab, the place of death, graves, and idolatry. The other path leads to bread and life in Bethlehem. Boaz, the worship of Yahweh, and the covenant community are in Bethlehem. The Bible depicts repentance as a *turning* away from sin to the Lord. When God's people fall into sin, he says to them, "*Return* to me." To what place will the characters in this story return?

For the time being, the three of them are on their way to Judah. Twice, in verses 6 and 7, we are told that Naomi arose and set out away from Moab toward Judah. Why does she do this? It is here that we continue to see God's goodness to her: "Then she arose with her daughters-in-law to return to the country of Moab for she had heard in the fields of Moab that the Lord had visited his people and given them food" (v. 6). Naomi and her husband had tried to build a life in Moab. Then, after the death of her husband and sons, Naomi was in the fields of Moab, presumably working there, when she heard the good news: the famine was over, there was food again in Bethlehem. Thus, a message got to Naomi somehow and the content of the message is this: "The Lord had visited his people and given them food." God made it rain and he caused fruit and wheat to grow for his people. The Bible affirms that God is the ultimate cause behind all the weather and all of our gifts, food, jobs, life, breath, and everything (Acts 17:24–25). We see this clearly taught in Job: "Behold, God is great, and we know him not; the number of his years is unsearchable. For he draws up the drops of water; they distill his mist in the rain, which the skies pour down and drop on mankind abundantly" (Job 36:26–28).

Our God is the God who gives and takes away. Sometimes, when he takes away, we forget that he gives, and gives continuously. He has given us his Son; how then will he not give us all things? (Rom 8:32). Because of God's goodness, Naomi hears news about Bethlehem and it is good news. But the other aspect of God's goodness we see here is that the Israelites

---

3. Ferguson, *Faithful God*, 20–21.

Part I: Emptiness and Loyalty

were still "his people" (Ruth 1:6).[4] The Lord had visited *his people* despite Israel's unfaithfulness at this time. God still regarded them as his own and he provided for them. This was so because he is good. He is *abundant* in goodness, as the Westminster Larger Catechism states it.[5] For Naomi, the Almighty had dealt bitterly with her. But she was a daughter in the covenant and, therefore, God had her eternal good in mind. Though he had, in fact, dealt bitterly with her, he meant *good* for her, in the end. But not *only* for her, as we will see.

So, the three women are on their way to Judah. Somewhere along the way Naomi thinks about the possible future her daughters-in-law might have with her in Judah. As she does this, Naomi breaks the silence and begins to speak to the two women. This dialogue between Naomi and the two women, and then between Naomi and Ruth, is what will be considered in this chapter and in subsequent chapters, as well. It should be noted that the bond between these three women was apparently quite strong. In verse 9, Naomi gives both of them a potential goodbye kiss, and they all weep. The deaths of their husbands in Moab permanently altered their lives and their relationship with one another. This might be the point where they, in turn, must say a final goodbye to Naomi. In this speech, Naomi's opinion is very clear. She says to her daughters-in-law, "Go, return, each of you" (v. 8). They were travelling to Judah and Naomi does not ask them to simply *think* about this other option. She *commands* them to return to Moab. Why did she do this? According to Naomi, the future of these two Moabite women in the land of Judah was very bleak. If they continued with her then their lives would undoubtedly be tied to Naomi's life. We see this possible future in Ruth's statement in verse 17: "Where you die, I will die and there will I be buried." For Naomi, the lives of these women attached to her own life was not a good thing. In Judah, according to Naomi, Orpah and Ruth would likely remain single. They could possibly catch more of Naomi's bitterness. And Naomi cares about them. She says to them, "Go back to Moab," and then she prays for them: "May the Lord deal kindly with you . . . the Lord grant that you may find rest" (vv. 8–9). The Hebrew word behind the phrase "deal kindly" here is *hesed*.[6] This word will come up again in this book. The word may be translated as "kindness" or "steadfast love." It is a rich word,

---

4. Block, *Judges, Ruth*, 631.
5. Westminster, "Larger Catechism," Q&A 7.
6. The word may be translated as "loyalty" or "faithfulness." Holladay, *Concise*, 111; Ferguson, *Faithful God*, 55–56; Block, *Judges, Ruth*, 633–34.

the meaning of which is difficult to get across in English. We may follow Ferguson here who defines *hesed* like this: "It means God's deep goodness expressed in his covenant commitment, his absolute loyalty, his obligating of himself to bring to fruition the blessings that he has promised, *whatever it may cost him personally to do that*."[7]

Naomi prays that *this* kind of love from God would be shown to these women. However, in her mind, this divine love *cannot* be found in Judah. We would do well to notice exactly *how* Naomi thinks that this prayer might be answered for them back in Moab: "The LORD grant that you may find rest, each of you in the house of her husband!" (v. 9). Naomi assumes that marriage to a man is the proper route for these women if they were to find "rest." To put it another way, faithful husbands would be an answer to her prayer here. This is a significant point for Christian men and women today. The context in which this prayer comes is one in which the men in the story, up to this point, are lacking in strength and integrity. The names Mahlon and Chilion could be understood as meaning something like "weak" and "sickly" respectively.[8] Many men in Israel were doing whatever they felt was right in their own eyes, leaving them *spiritually* sick and weak. Naomi said this prayer as an Israelite woman living "in the days that the judges ruled" (v. 1). We could go back to the book of Judges, which reveals what these days were like in Israel. A stark record of the horrific consequences of male abuse and indiscretion, even among God's own people at this time, is given toward the end of Judges. A woman is murdered, and this results in a vicious war among the tribes within Israel. For the Christian man, here we are reminded of what he, by God's grace, is to strive *not* to be. If he is married, rest is what he seeks to provide for his wife. If single, and desiring marriage, he is to prepare himself now so that he might be the kind of man who is able to give rest to a woman such as Ruth. For the Christian woman, despite the weaknesses and abuses of men in the unbelieving culture, and even within the church at times, she is to continue to be patient, remain faithful, and she is to trust in the LORD that rest is attainable in the house of a faithful husband. Christian marriage will always be a target of Satan's schemes, whether he launches his attacks from the surrounding pagan culture or from within the marriage itself, in the hearts and minds of husband and wife. Men and women in the church are to be on guard against this,

---

7. Ferguson, *Faithful God*, 56.
8. Block and Hubbard both argue that the meanings are uncertain. Block, *Judges, Ruth*, 625; Hubbard, *Book of Ruth*, 89–90. See also Ferguson, *Faithful God*, 23.

praying that our homes would be places of rest for all those within. Above all, for men and women, single or married, we are *all* to remember that true rest is ultimately found in the church's one bridegroom, Jesus Christ.

Marriage is a good thing, one in which husband and wife, as they remain faithful to God's word, may experience the steadfast love, the *hesed*, of our Savior and have rest. The book of Ruth ends with a marriage. The Bible ends with a marriage (Rev 19:6–8). For Naomi, she seems to still be thinking along similar lines, that marriage is good. So, she prays that God would give these women husbands. But she thinks this will only be able to happen in Moab, which is why she also tells them to return. We are able to see how Naomi somewhat distances herself from God here: "May the LORD deal kindly with you." In other words, *if* good things from God are still available to this family, they will surely come upon the other two women, *not* Naomi. In Naomi's mind, God has proven how he will be with her. Perhaps there is some good yet to be found for someone else, though, like these two daughters-in-law of hers. We have seen that Naomi prays that God would show these women covenant love or covenant faithfulness, *hesed*. We will come to find out that Boaz is an answer to this prayer for Ruth. While Naomi is attempting to distance herself from the LORD, he is drawing her back to himself by answering her prayer.

What will be seen in this book is that just as Boaz was an expression of God's steadfast love for Ruth and Naomi, Jesus is the *ultimate* expression of God's steadfast love to *all* his people. It is in him, a crucified and risen Savior, that we find rest, permanent rest. We see Christ's shadow appear already here in the land. The land itself experienced a kind of resurrection from death. Food from the ground is produced again in Judah. There is abundant fruit when there once was famine. Through this resurrection of the land the LORD was drawing Naomi and Ruth to himself. This is what he does for every one of us in the church. God has raised his Son from the dead. Even in the midst of much suffering, as we continue to go on our way, the LORD leads us toward *him*, toward resurrection life. Naomi was heading toward Judah, thinking that she would live out the rest of her life there, a lonely and bitter woman. But she was heading toward so much more.

Chapter 3: A Daughter Clings

RUTH 1:10-14

And they said to her, "No, we will return with you to your people." But Naomi said, "Turn back, my daughters; why will you go with me? Have I yet sons in my womb that they may become your husbands? Turn back, my daughters; go your way, for I am too old to have a husband. If I should say I have hope, even if I should have a husband this night and should bear sons, would you therefore wait till they were grown? Would you therefore refrain from marrying? No, my daughters, for it is exceedingly bitter to me for your sake that the hand of the Lord has gone out against me." Then they lifted up their voices and wept again. And Orpah kissed her mother-in-law, but Ruth clung to her.

THE LAST SOUND WE heard from Ruth and Orpah was weeping. Naomi, while on their way to Judah, had stopped and insisted that they both turn around and travel back to Moab. These three women had experienced much sorrow during their years together in Moab. All three of their husbands had died. Where would they find rest? Naomi thinks that these women should remarry and find rest in the houses of their husbands. But Naomi thinks new husbands will *not* be found in Judah. So, she urges them both to leave her and return to Moab. What was in Moab? After Orpah decides to return to Moab, this is what Naomi says to Ruth: "See your sister-in-law has gone back to her people and to her gods; return after your sister-in-law" (v. 15). We have already seen in this story that Moab was the place of graves. These

Part I: Emptiness and Loyalty

women buried three husbands there. It was a place where multiple gods were worshiped, as can be seen from Naomi's words to Ruth about Orpah: "Your sister-in-law has gone back . . . to her gods." Though we are not told what becomes of Orpah, Moab is a symbol of death and darkness, a place where idols are worshiped. The darkness of Moab had swallowed up the men in this family. Three Israelite men returned to the dust in Moab. These three widows are now faced with an important question to answer in regard to their lives. Where will they place their hope for a future?

For Naomi, it was natural for her to physically return to Judah. She was an Israelite, of the blood of Abraham. Whether or not she would trust God *from her heart* was another matter. But at this point, it seems appropriate for her to return to her people in Judah. But these other two women, they are Moabite women. They were, by definition, outside the covenant. They were part of a people that was pagan, unclean, and whose sins mounted up to heaven. To be associated with them was to become defiled by them: "No Ammonite or Moabite may enter the assembly of the Lord. . . . You shall not seek their peace or their prosperity all your days forever" (Deut 23:3, 6). The incorporation of these two women into the covenant community of Israel had, on some level, already happened through their marriages to the two Israelite men in Moab, Naomi's sons. But without their Israelite husbands, the decision to press on and live out their days *in the land of Israel* takes on a whole new level of seriousness and devotion.

At first, these two women speak with one voice in response to Naomi's initial command to return: "And they said to her, 'No, we will return with you to your people'" (Ruth 1:10). But Naomi comes right back, insistent that for her daughters-in-law, their only hope for a future in the house of a husband would be found in Moab, among Moabite men. Twice, Naomi says to them "turn back" (vv. 11–12). This repeated phrase translates a form of the same word, *shub*, which is also rendered as "return" in this chapter. She then dreams up a scenario as to how her daughters-in-law *might* find husbands in Judah. She follows this by carefully crafting her language in a such a way as to show them how a husband would be impossible to find on this path.[1] For Naomi, she can only think of one way these women would find men and that was through her. She says, "Even if I should have a husband this night and should bear sons, would you therefore wait till they are grown? Would you therefore refrain from marrying?" (vv. 12–13). Naomi was asking Ruth and Orpah something like this: "Would you be able to

---

1. Hubbard, *Book of Ruth*, 108–11.

subdue your passions and desires for twenty years until the boys are old enough?" By that time the women would likely be well past child-bearing age (assuming of course Naomi did in fact have *sons*, not daughters). This is a ridiculous prospect. Aside from this, Naomi had already ruled out this option: "I am too old to have a husband" (v. 12). Naomi sought to suffocate any hope for finding a husband in Judah out of their minds so that she might be left to reenter Bethlehem alone.

We will come to find out that Naomi had apparently forgotten about not just one but *two* family members, Boaz and another man, who had the legal right ("legal" in regard to Old Testament law) to redeem the bloodline of Naomi's husband, Elimelech. She will find out soon enough that she does not have to miraculously provide a husband, for Ruth at least, from her own womb. Boaz is in the wings. In fact, during this conversation on the way to Judah, he was most likely working in the fields (now fruitful) with his workers. Naomi, it seems, has tunnel vision. She cannot seem to look past her own bitterness. And so, she tries to isolate herself. She attempts to do this again when she gets back to Bethlehem. The community asks about her well-being and Naomi responds with this: "Do not call me Naomi; call me Mara" (v. 20). It is the bitterness of loss and disappointment that has Naomi attempting to push others away.

In these interchanges Naomi is loud. Her words dominate the space through verse 14. She is insistent. She says to them two times to "turn back," and then follows this up by flat out saying "No" in verse 13. Although determined to convince both of them to go back to Moab, Naomi nevertheless reveals the close bond that existed between them. She calls Ruth and Orpah "my daughters" (v. 13). And yet, she still attempts to push them both away. We should take notice here of how Naomi uses her words to talk about the relationship between herself, the Lord, and these two Moabite women. In verse 13 she says, "No, my daughters, for it is exceedingly bitter to me for your sake that the hand of the Lord has gone out against me." Essentially, she is answering this question: "What kind of relationship does *Naomi* have with the Lord?" And her answer is this: "The hand of the Lord has gone out against me." This is a phrase used similarly elsewhere in Holy Scripture to refer to divine judgment against sin (Exod 9:3; Deut 2:15; Judg 2:15).[2] She refers to God being exceedingly bitter toward her by his most recent actions. But she adds "for your sake" in the middle of this, which is to say something like this: "This bitterness is mine, go your way." The listener

---

2. I am indebted to Block for these references. *Judges, Ruth*, 637.

PART I: EMPTINESS AND LOYALTY

might be asking himself at this point, "Had not God taken away Ruth and Orpah's husbands as well?" Naomi doesn't mention that here. To be sure, they were Naomi's sons, but these women before her are suffering as well.

Orpah is convinced. She heeds Naomi's entreaties and commands. She does *return* to Moab. In the last verse of this section, we see the two Moabite women acting in unison for the last time in this story. They had each been incorporated, on some level, into the fellowship with the covenant community of Israel through marriage to Jewish men, albeit in *Moab*. They had both lost these men. They both wept and they initially responded to Naomi with one voice, refusing to leave her: "No, we will return with you to your people" (Ruth 1:10). And finally, in verse 14, they lift their voices up *together* and weep again. It is at this point, however, that a separation begins. Orpah *alone* is mentioned. She *alone* gives her mother-in-law a goodbye kiss. She *alone* will return to Moab.

But what about Ruth? What about *this* widowed daughter-in-law? What about *this* woman from Moab? By the providence of God, she has been plucked out of Moabite culture and drawn into the Israelite way of life through her former husband—now dead—and now through Naomi. What will *she* do? The decision has to be hers. Orpah cannot make it for her. Naomi cannot make it for her. She is confronted with a monumental decision. This section ends with two silent actions from Orpah and Ruth. Orpah kisses Naomi. And it is a goodbye kiss. It is a kiss given before she turns back to her old Moabite culture and world. Will Ruth do the same? She will not. The last line shows, by her silent action, what was in her heart. In a moment, she will confess this with her mouth. But for now, we are only told this: "But Ruth clung to her" (v. 14). Ruth cleaved herself to Naomi.[3]

Ruth's clinging to Naomi was most likely a physical clinging. We are not told this explicitly, nor are we told in what manner Ruth clung to her. Perhaps she wrapped her arms around Naomi's neck. Maybe she was on her knees at the feet of Naomi. Maybe she was standing directly in front of Naomi, clinging to her hands, with a strong look of determination in her eyes, as she talked eye-to-eye with her mother-in-law. We do not know for sure. It seems likely that this was a physical embrace of some kind since we are told, by contrast, that Orpah *kissed* Naomi goodbye. We are also told, after Ruth's verbal confession, that Naomi "saw that she was determined to go with her" (v. 18). Whether or not Ruth *physically* clung to her

---

3. Holladay, *Concise*, 66; Hubbard, *Book of Ruth*, 115.

Chapter 3: A Daughter Clings

mother-in-law, the text makes it abundantly clear that, in contrast with Orpah, Ruth was not turning back to Moab. Ruth, instead, *clung* to Naomi.

The word translated here, "clung," is the same word used by Moses in the book of Genesis to describe the bond of marriage. It is translated there as "hold fast": "Therefore a man shall leave his father and his mother and hold fast to his wife, and they shall become one flesh" (Gen 2:24). Our passage from Ruth (1:14), of course, is not referring to marriage, a covenant between one man and one woman. But Ruth does "cling" or "hold fast" to Naomi with a similar *type* of covenant loyalty, self-sacrifice, and commitment that is seen in a faithful marriage bond. It is not Naomi, the woman, essentially, to whom Ruth clings, although for Ruth, this *is* part of what is happening here. It is ultimately to Naomi's God and to Naomi's people that Ruth cleaves herself. Again, this action is in contrast to what Orpah has done, returning to the people of Moab and to the gods of Moab. *If* Ruth is to find true hope in a dismal situation, she will find it in covenant with Yahweh, the Lord God of Israel, and in lifelong fellowship with his people. And she will do this, regardless of how bitter this *natural born* Israelite woman she clings to seems to be. In the context overall, if we consider the blessings of God given to Naomi and her people in history—namely, his word, the promise of a Messiah, the atoning sacrifices, etc.—as opposed to God's dealings with the Moabites, Ruth's heartfelt conviction here *should* have been seen in Naomi.

What is Naomi to Ruth at this moment? Would it not be appropriate to consider Naomi as a kind of symbol of the church for Ruth? Through Naomi, and her people, this Moabite woman will hear about the promises of God. Clinging to Naomi, Ruth will witness the sacrifices being made. She will later hear more about the Messiah. She will experience, on some level, Israel's *religious* life. In *this* way, by continually clinging to Naomi and her people, Ruth will take refuge under the wings of Almighty God. Boaz will affirm this about Ruth later in chapter 2, when he confesses part of what he found to be attractive in her:

> All that you have done for your mother-in-law since the death of your husband has been fully told to me, and how you left your father and mother and your native land and came to a people that you did not know before. The Lord repay you for what you have done, and a full reward be given you by the Lord, the God of Israel, under whose wings you have come to take refuge! (2:11–12)

Part I: Emptiness and Loyalty

For Christians, this is what the church, the *true* church, is to us. It is in the context of Christ's body, including first our own families and then from there the members of the local church, that the Christian life is lived out. It is in the church and through the church that God reveals his mercy in the gospel. For the gospel teaches us about the cross, where the hand of the Lord went out against God's own Son, Jesus Christ, for the sins of his people, the church. The church is not just a collection of like-minded people, nor is it merely a social club. The church, by the power of the Holy Spirit, is *the body of Christ*. We could lay the emphasis elsewhere in order to get this point across: the church *is* the body of Christ. We would do well to really appreciate this permanent spiritual reality. In clinging to the church by faith, believers, in a very real way, cling to Jesus Christ. The Westminster Confession of Faith defines the church in this way: "The catholic or universal church, which is invisible, consists of the whole number of the elect, that have been, are, or shall be gathered into one, under Christ the head thereof; and is the spouse, the body, the fullness of him that filleth all in all."[4] In the midst of exceeding bitterness in this life, this is where true hope is found for believers: in committed, loving fellowship with other brothers and sisters in Christ, in the context of a local body where the promises of the gospel are faithfully proclaimed week in and week out on the Lord's Day. It is in the hearing of the gospel, and receiving the sacraments of baptism and the Lord's supper, within the gathered worship of God's people, that believers *cling* to Jesus Christ. We have one Spirit—the Spirit of Christ—who dwells within us and who will never leave us nor forsake us. It is this self-same Spirit who was at work in Ruth, here, as she clung to the only symbol of hope for her at this point in her life—Naomi, of Bethlehem in Judah.

---

4. Westminster, "Confession of Faith," 25:1.

Chapter 4: A Daughter Confesses

RUTH 1:15-18

And she said, "See, your sister-in-law has gone back to her people and to her gods; return after your sister-in-law." But Ruth said, "Do not urge me to leave you or to return from following you. For where you go I will go, and where you lodge I will lodge. Your people shall be my people, and your God my God. Where you die I will die, and there will I be buried. May the LORD do so to me and more also if anything but death parts me from you." And when Naomi saw that she was determined to go with her, she said no more.

THIS SECTION CENTERS ON Ruth's confession. The words that Ruth speaks here make up one of the most beautiful parts of Scripture. In terms of the elegance, symmetry, and power that this young widowed Moabite woman packs into a few words, there are not many places in the Bible that match it.[1] These are the words of Ruth, in the power of the Spirit. And so, we see the beauty and perfection of the Spirit come through here in a special and memorable way.

Ruth's confession is framed by descriptions of what Naomi does. The section begins with more of Naomi's urging of Ruth to follow her sister-in-law in returning to Moab. And the section ends with a reference to Naomi's change of heart and her silence. In verse 15, Orpah has left the group to go back to Moab. Ruth is clinging to Naomi still, apparently. Naomi sees this and is still insistent that Ruth return. If we consider the symmetry of

1. Block, *Judges, Ruth*, 640.

Part I: Emptiness and Loyalty

Naomi's statement to Ruth here, we might see that Naomi's words are somewhat poetic as well: "See, your sister-in-law has gone back to her people and to her gods; return after your sister-in-law." Here, then, is the logical pattern: sister-in-law, return, return, sister-in-law. Naomi produces a kind of mirror image in the last part of what she says in the first part.[2] Additionally, she inserts a reference to the other sister-in-law's gods and her people. Even though Naomi is still making the argument that Ruth should stop following her, it seems to be less forceful than her earlier remarks. Ruth is clinging to her after all. Really, from a literary standpoint, the writer uses these last words from Naomi to Ruth to set up what Ruth says in response. Though Naomi's statement has repetition and symmetry, Ruth's powerful plea back to Naomi completely overshadows Naomi's words. Ruth's confession takes center stage.

Naomi had her chance to speak and make her argument. Now it is Ruth's turn. And she does so with nearly matchless poetry. Her confession is made up of five two-line couplets.[3] The five pairs of lines center upon, and therefore emphasize, the second part of verse 16. This is the third pair and the clear centerpoint of Ruth's speech: "Your people shall be my people, and your God my God." We could structure the lines in the way below to provide a visual representation of this powerful, poetic balance.[4] Here, one may see more clearly how the first two couplets correspond with their mirrored couplets on the opposite side of the speech (*A* and *A'*—"leaving and parting"; *B* and *B'*—"going/lodging and dying/burial"):

> *A*   Do not urge me to leave you
> or to return from following you
> > *B*   For where you go I will go
> > and where you lodge I will lodge.
> > > *C*   Your people shall be my people,
> > > *C*   and your God my God.
> > *B'*   Where you die I will die,
> > and there will I be buried.
> *A'*   May the Lord do so to me and more also
> if anything but death parts me from you.

---

2. It should be noted here that in the original Hebrew the word order is technically this: "return, sister-in-law, return, sister-in-law." Even if viewed this way, the poetic reflection is still evident.

3. Block, *Judges, Ruth*, 640–41.

4. Block, *Judges, Ruth*, 640.

Chapter 4: A Daughter Confesses

We see here that she even borrows from Naomi's initial speech: "Back to her people and to her gods" (1:15). To which Ruth essentially replies, "No, I am going with *your* people and to *your* God." Ruth's words, in fact, are so powerful that once she finishes speaking, Naomi is silenced: "And when Naomi saw that she was determined to go with her, she said no more" (v. 18). The phrase translated as "she was determined to go" does not quite get across the kind of immovable conviction that Naomi saw in Ruth. The text, more woodenly translated, says something like "she saw Ruth had *strengthened herself* to go with her."[5] Naomi, then, kept her mouth shut. Ruth, at this point, was a pillar of faith. Not even one of God's chosen people (Naomi from the nation of Israel) could change her mind. (Would that we all had conviction like this!) Matthew includes Ruth in his genealogy of Christ, alongside Mary, Rahab, and Tamar. These women are presented in Scripture as having *strong* faith. Men reading this story would do well to learn from this formidable figure in redemptive history—the woman Ruth.

Again, the section begins with Naomi's last effort to convince Ruth to return from following her and it ends with Naomi being finally silenced. The majority of the section is taken up by Ruth's extraordinary speech. Ruth first says, "Do not urge me to leave you, or to return from following you" (v. 16). Thus she begins her speech to Naomi with a command of her own, and the command begins in the negative: "Do not urge me to leave you." This language of leaving and returning from following after another is similar to the covenant promise that God himself gave to Joshua not long before these events took place within Elimelech's family. When Israel was about to enter the promised land for the first time under the leadership of Joshua, God said to Joshua, "I will not leave you or forsake you" (Josh 1:5). Ruth says, "Do not urge me to leave you or to return from following you." God also said to Joshua, "Be strong and courageous" (Josh 1:6, 9). This is exactly what Ruth is doing here. She is being strong and courageous. Her actions and her sincere confession testify to this.

The next three lines make up Ruth's positive commitment to Naomi: "For where you go I will go, and where you lodge I will lodge. Your people shall be my people, and your God my God. Where you die I will die, and there will I be buried." Ruth continues to use the same covenantal language God has used with Israel in the history of his relationship to his people, as will be seen. But first, we may consider that in this confession, Ruth's separation from Orpah, and by extension Moab and the Moabite religious

---

5. Hubbard, *Book of Ruth*, 121.

culture, is nearing completion. Ruth makes references to essentially every stage in a person's life. "Going" might be a reference to a kind of general weekly activity while "lodging" clearly refers to a settled existence in a home or homes, and this, in a particular land. Ruth even looks past all of this to death and burial after death. According to Ruth, from now on, the life of Naomi the Israelite and Ruth the woman from Moab will be permanently tied together, even in death. She wants to be buried in Israel, in Naomi's family plot even: "there will I be buried."[6] We would do well to notice the complete shift here. Ruth had started on this journey toward Judah loosely associated with the other Moabite woman, Orpah. They lifted up their voices and wept *together* (Ruth 1:9). They both initially said that they wanted to return with Naomi to Bethlehem (v. 10). But Ruth and Orpah begin to separate, as Orpah leaves while Ruth *clings* to Naomi. We are reminded here of what must happen for *every one* of God's people. Christianity is not simply saying the sinner's prayer (although something like this may be part of one's conversion). It is not simply a culture nor is it to be associated, primarily, with any political party or movement. Christianity is a *life*. To be sure, it is a life built on belief in right doctrine. But belief in the Scriptural doctrine of the gospel empowers and shapes that life. And it is a life lived primarily in war against sin. As Ruth mentions here, our going and lodging, and even our dying, as a Christian, are all to be done in commitment to the LORD our God, with whom we have living fellowship through faith in Christ. As the apostle Paul says, "Whether we eat or whether we drink, we are to do it all to the glory of God" (1 Cor 10:31).

This is the kind of life Ruth envisioned while *clinging* to Naomi. Whether she lived or whether she died, she would live and die to the LORD in loving fellowship with Naomi and her people. We can notice the repeated references from Ruth's lips about her view of the relationship she has with her mother-in-law: "Where you go I will go ... where you lodge I will lodge ... where you die I will die" (Ruth 1:16–17). "You and I, you and I, you and I" is the refrain alongside also claiming what is "yours and mine": "Your people shall be my people and your God my God" (v. 16). Earlier Naomi, the Israelite, had prayed to God that he would give Ruth and Orpah rest. In this prayer she meant God-granted rest in finding a husband in Moab. Ruth also calls upon God but in a different way. In verse 17, she makes what is essentially a formal oath or vow. She says, "May the LORD do so to me and more also if anything but death parts me from you." Ruth was calling upon

---

6. Block, *Judges, Ruth*, 641; Hubbard, *Book of Ruth*, 118.

Chapter 4: A Daughter Confesses

God, the God of Israel, to act as a witness in what she had just confessed.[7] The idea, then, would be that if Ruth's confession proved insincere or if she broke her promise by separating from Naomi *before* death separated them, then God himself would bring down divine curses on Ruth's head for breaking her promise. What this shows is that as far as Ruth was able to perceive what was going on in her own heart and spirit, she was sincere. So much so that she considered her commitment and confession serious enough to warrant making an oath such as this. There is a lesson here for us that we *all* would take our vows, our oaths, our words, and our faith this seriously.

If we are honest with ourselves, we would easily recognize times when we have not lived up to the standard of commitment Ruth sets here. We may, then, be able to understand more clearly why Naomi doesn't speak again after this speech. There is really no arguing with the structure, sincerity, and power displayed in these words. The most important part of Ruth's speech is found right in the middle—couplet C. The words in verse 16 are translated in English as "Your people shall be my people, and your God my God." In the original, the line consists of only four Hebrew words, and none of them are verbs. In the rest of her commitment to Naomi there are verbs: leave, go, lodge, die, and bury. But in the middle couplet, a word for word translation reads this way: "Your people, my people, your God, my God." The separation is complete. Ruth refuses to return to Moab because she has forever turned body and soul to Israel and to Israel's God.

The language that Ruth uses in this central couplet is again strongly reminiscent of the covenant language God used with Israel. She says, "Your people shall be my people and your God my God." Compare this with what the LORD said to Moses prior to Israel's great deliverance from slavery in Egypt: "I will redeem you with an outstretched arm and with great acts of judgment. I will take you to be my people and I will be your God and you will know I am the LORD your God" (Exod 6:6–7). How does Ruth know to speak this way about Israel's God? It is probable that Ruth had some exposure to the Jewish Scriptures through her husband and her husband's family. She may have been introduced to the Old Testament promises given through Moses and so spoke to Naomi in a similar vein. Ultimately, however, it was the Spirit, the Spirit of Christ, who put these words on her lips. That was the purpose for covenanting with Israel and redeeming her in the first place: that God might put the confession of his name in the mouths of

---

7. Block, *Judges, Ruth*, 642.

Part I: Emptiness and Loyalty

people from *all* nations, even Moab. Ruth here is a foreshadowing of this worldwide work of God through Christ (Gen 12:1–3; 18:17–18. More on this below).

What Scripture reveals later on is that God had grafted Ruth into Israel, *so that* he might bring a king into the world through Boaz's genealogical line. Ruth would give birth to a son of Boaz of Bethlehem in Judah. This son, Obed, born to Boaz and Ruth, would turn out to be the grandfather of David, the king of Israel (Ruth 4:20–21). Therefore, a descendent of Judah would be king just as God had promised. And this king would suffer to bring glory to God's name. David suffered much for God's glory as the king of Israel. But his suffering was but a type of a greater suffering from a greater king to come. Jesus said this in regard to the essence of Old Testament teaching, including the book of Ruth: "Thus it is written, that the Christ should suffer and on the third day rise from the dead, and that repentance for the forgiveness should be proclaimed in his name to all nations" (Luke 24:46–47). Jesus is this promised Messianic King.

Bringing Jesus into the world was the God-ordained *result* of drawing Ruth into the fellowship of Israel. But what was the *cause*? What propelled this Moabite woman to confess her covenant loyalty to Naomi's people and Naomi's God in words spoken with such arresting beauty? Towering, like a long shadow, over the lives of these women in this story, up to this point, was the death of Elimelech, of the tribe of Judah. This was followed, of course, by the deaths of his sons. But it is Elimelech who is mentioned by name four more times in the rest of the story following this section (Ruth 2:1, 3; 4:3, 9). Boaz had significance for Naomi and Ruth precisely because he was "of the clan of Elimelech" (2:1). Thus, if we widen our perspective somewhat, the answer to the questions above could be stated in this way: God sovereignly brought Ruth to this point and placed this confession on her lips *by way of* the death of a man from the tribe of Judah.[8] Is this not what God has been doing for nearly two thousand years since his Son came to earth, placing the confession of his name on believing gentiles from all over the world? He has. And behind these Spirit-wrought confessions is the death of a man from the tribe of Judah. *This* man was, and is, not just any man, though. He is the Son of God made flesh, Jesus Christ. In the book of Revelation, he is referred to as "the Lion of the tribe of Judah" (Rev 5:5). This God-man of the tribe of Judah was slain like a lamb so that those who believe in him, from every tribe and nation, might share in Ruth's

---

8. Ferguson writes, "It is a gospel secret that death is the way to life." *Faithful God*, 38.

CHAPTER 4: A DAUGHTER CONFESSES

Spirit-produced conviction and say to Jesus, our Lord: "You are my God, your people are my people."

Chapter 5: Arriving Home

RUTH 1:19–22

So the two of them went on until they came to Bethlehem. And when they came to Bethlehem, the whole town was stirred because of them. And the women said, "Is this Naomi?" She said to them, "Do not call me Naomi; call me Mara, for the Almighty has dealt very bitterly with me. I went away full, and the Lord has brought me back empty. Why call me Naomi, when the Lord has testified against me and the Almighty has brought calamity upon me?"
So Naomi returned, and Ruth the Moabite her daughter-in-law with her, who returned from the country of Moab. And they came to Bethlehem at the beginning of barley harvest.

The section that closes chapter 1 ends on a somewhat negative note. After such a mesmerizing confession by Ruth in the previous verses, the reader is left, still, with more questions after the end of the chapter. It is obvious Naomi is still bitter. But she is back in Bethlehem, where there is food again. And now Ruth, a Moabite, is with her. Ruth has promised to die with Naomi. Now that she has arrived in Judah with Naomi, this is where Ruth's confession will be put to the test. It is one thing to make such a strong confession on the way to Bethlehem, when it was just her and Naomi. Now, though, she is faced with a city that is "stirred" as a result of Naomi and Ruth's arrival. And this jostled city is full of Jewish women asking questions about Naomi. She has vowed lifelong commitment to Naomi, who is now essentially laying accusations upon the God of Israel. And she is doing this

Chapter 5: Arriving Home

publicly! Naomi says here, "The Lord has brought me back empty" (v. 21). What about Ruth? Doesn't Naomi have her? In her own mind, Naomi is so "empty" that this statement could be taken as a rebuke against her own daughter-in-law. Having a Moabite daughter committed to her in life and in death is not enough for Naomi to consider her life as full. "No," Naomi says, "I am returning empty."

The text is abrupt in its summary of Ruth and Naomi's return to Bethlehem. After the famine in Bethlehem, the move to Moab, the marriages and deaths in Moab, and the dramatic verbal interchanges between Orpah, Ruth, and Naomi, all the writer says in verse 19 is this: "So the two of them went on until they came to Bethlehem." We believe this to be purposeful. This flat and concise summary of Ruth and Naomi's return sets up Naomi's final retort against God. The last thing that Naomi had said about Yahweh was "The hand of the Lord has gone out against me" (v. 13). Ruth, by her confession and by clinging to Naomi, had made it clear to Naomi that she was *not* listening. Ruth had made up her mind. Naomi needed to find a new audience upon whom to volley her complaints against God. She finds this in Bethlehem. If Ruth will not confirm her bitterness, maybe these women in Bethlehem will. So, we are introduced to a new setting and a new dialogue.

Naomi and Ruth enter Bethlehem and like circling a spoon in a cup of tea, their arrival stirs up the people: "The whole town was stirred because of them" (v. 19). Why were they stirred? Notice that the text talks about the whole city being agitated, but then it is the women who speak: "And the women said, 'Is this Naomi?'" (v. 19). So, this group of women take special interest in Naomi's return. They are familiar enough with Naomi to ask this question and to call her by name. These women show up again at the end of the story, after Ruth gives birth to Naomi's grandson: "Then the women said to Naomi, 'Blessed be the Lord, who has not left you this day without a redeemer and may his name be renowned in Israel'" (4:14). The fact that this is a *group* of women speaking puts emphasis on the contents of their speech. And what they say together here directs our attention, once again, to Naomi: "Is this Naomi?" This question is not like hearing a familiar voice in the background of a phone conversation and the speaker asks, "Is that Mom in the background?" These women are saying the question in a manner more like this: "Is *this* Naomi?"

It is possible the townspeople in Bethlehem heard of Naomi's plight. It had been ten years since Naomi had left Bethlehem with her husband and her two sons. She is now ten years older, but she had experienced much suffering in those ten years. And she had just returned from a journey of significant distance. We are not told this, but Naomi's physical appearance may have changed. The bitterness she complains about may have aged her significantly. However, even if this was not the case, Naomi does return *without* her husband and *without* her sons. She has a daughter-in-law with her but the loss of her husband and her two sons is serious. The question, "Is this Naomi?" would, then, be focusing on her widowhood and her childlessness.

Men, particularly sons, were important in an Israelite family because it was through them that the *name* of the family was continued through time and history. This is what Boaz mentions to the other redeemer in the story. He asks that man if he wanted to take Ruth to be his wife. The reason he gave this offer was to "perpetuate the name of the dead in his inheritance" (4:5). Since Elimelech and his two sons died, the name of Elimelech in the tribe of Judah would also die, or would be "cut off from among his brothers" (4:10) when Naomi and Ruth died (if they did not remarry and have children). Along with the name was the inheritance. The portion of land and the property that normally would stay in the family line would be passed to someone else once Naomi and Ruth died. In addition to this, God promised Israel that he would give them a royal figure *through* the family bloodline of Judah. He also promised the nations would be blessed *through the seed* of Abraham. If Elimelech's blood line disappeared, could it be that other family lines could die as well? Could it be that the name of Israel itself would be "blotted out" from world history entirely? With these questions in mind, one might see more clearly why Naomi considered herself "empty." Perhaps *all* of Israel felt this way as well, "in the days when the judges ruled." Regardless of what the nation as a whole may have felt, Naomi should have continued to trust wholeheartedly in God's word. His word prevails, irrespective of what our interpretations of the circumstances might be.

But Naomi is bitter. The women of Bethlehem ask the question, "Is this Naomi?" The mention of her name, which means "pleasant," prompts Naomi to request that she not be called by that name anymore. Instead, she wants to be called Mara, which means "bitter," because of the bitterness God caused her: "Do not call me Naomi; call me Mara" (v. 20). In *her* testimony about God, which is set against Ruth's confession here, Naomi pits herself against God. To her, it seems now that God has become like an adversary to her. We may consider how she goes back and forth between

Chapter 5: Arriving Home

the LORD and herself: "I went away full, and the LORD has brought me back empty. Why call me Naomi, when the LORD has testified against me and the Almighty has brought calamity upon me?" Four times she affirms that God is the ultimate cause for all of her troubles. Twice she refers to God as the LORD, using God's personal name, Yahweh. The other two times she refers to God as the Almighty, a name that emphasizes his power. In other words, the personal, covenant God of Israel had summoned his power in order to strike Naomi with a bitter blow.

It is abundantly clear that Naomi is indignant about her situation. While Ruth had just said to Naomi, "Your God shall be my God," thereby taking hold of the God of Israel as her shield and protector, Naomi seems to be hurling accusations at God. The language she uses is likened to that found in a judicial verdict. God had found Naomi guilty and punished her accordingly. Naomi is wrongheaded here. She had suffered much, to be sure, but at this point the reader might be ready to shut his ears to her complaining. This final statement from Naomi in chapter 1 is a far cry from Job's statement in the midst of his tremendous suffering: "The LORD gave, and the LORD has taken away; blessed be the name of the LORD" (Job 1:21).

As wrongheaded as Naomi may have been, she does speak truth here. The LORD, the Almighty, is the ultimate cause behind everything that happens. *Every* life, *every* death, *every* occurrence, regardless of how seemingly random or chaotic in our eyes, falls out according to God's plan and purpose. Scripture teaches us that God "works all things according to the counsel of his will" (Eph 1:11). The Westminster Shorter Catechism summarizes the Bible's teaching on God's providence by stating that God, "for his own glory" has foreordained "whatsoever comes to pass."[1] The Almighty *did* put down Elimelech and his two sons. Looked at in this way, then, the LORD *did* strike Naomi for his wise purposes. And one of those purposes was to draw Ruth to himself. While Naomi is hurling accusations at God, Ruth is there in Bethlehem, physically present in the heart of Israel. Yes, the Almighty did these things, but the LORD did them for infinitely good and wise reasons, and one of these very *good* reasons was to save Ruth. She was the apple of his eye just as much as Naomi.

More than this though, the LORD did these things to bring Ruth to Bethlehem so that she might meet a particular man in Bethlehem, this family's redeemer. Through Ruth's womb and the line of Boaz, the LORD would bring the grandfather of a righteous king into Israel's dark world. Many

---

1. Westminster, "Shorter Catechism," Q&A 7.

Part I: Emptiness and Loyalty

generations later, Israel's Messiah and God's Son would assume a human nature and be born in Bethlehem. His family line can be traced back here to this story, to Boaz and Ruth. To put it another way, Jesus's birth was possible because of what God was doing here and because of what God had *purposed* in Naomi's life. Despite the personal bitterness, her words were true: the Lord, not blind chance or a dark fate, had brought calamity upon Naomi.

Jesus, who was to be born, many generations later, in the very town in which Naomi and Ruth were standing, was born in order that he might *die* at Calvary. This, too, was part of God's eternal plan. The Lord made him walk an exceedingly bitter path. Why did he do this? Like Ruth, who was taken from Moab and transferred into Bethlehem because of God's power and grace, so, too, all believers have been transferred into God's heavenly kingdom. Jesus thus endured the calamity brought upon him at the cross to redeem his elect from the penalty due to them for their sins. This happened, ultimately, not because of a decision his people autonomously made, but because the Lord God Almighty chose us in Christ before the foundation of the world. It is because of God's infinite wisdom and power that Ruth and Naomi were stirring up Bethlehem at this time. And it is because of God's wisdom and power that families in every generation are led to Christ, to the forgiveness of sins in him, and to his redeemed people. We should praise him for this, no matter what bitter path he makes us walk.

Lastly, we would do well to consider the fact that the Lord continues to do this in every generation. The story of Naomi and Ruth doesn't stop here. There is more to come. The last line of the chapter says that Naomi and Ruth returned to Judah at the beginning of barley harvest. Food is back in Bethlehem. A ripe harvest is waiting to be reaped and gathered into the barns of Israel. Ruth will be introduced to her redeemer husband in these harvest fields. Believers today have met their Redeemer Jesus, and they continue to meet with him in the hearing of the gospel in gathered worship each week. But there are some who have not met Christ. In the Gospel of John, we see Jesus comparing the souls of people in the world to a wheat harvest like the one mentioned in this section in Ruth: "Lift up your eyes, and see that the fields are white for harvest" (John 4:35). Therefore, the church should pray to the Lord of the harvest, that through the church, through the proclamation of the death of this son of Judah, Jesus the Christ, that God Almighty would sovereignly reap his resurrection harvest from these fields.

Chapter 5: Arriving Home

Our writer has us looking forward now. We have seen Naomi and Ruth go through much bitterness and pain. Naomi attempted to compel Ruth to look back to Moab. Naomi, in a sense, here in Bethlehem, is still looking back to what happened to her there. But brighter days are ahead. These golden fields are calling to Ruth, so she might meet her man: "And they came to Bethlehem at the beginning of barley harvest."

Part II: Ruth and Boaz

Chapter 1: An Introduction

RUTH 2:1-7

Now Naomi had a relative of her husband's, a worthy man of the clan of Elimelech, whose name was Boaz. And Ruth the Moabite said to Naomi, "Let me go to the field and glean among the ears of grain after him in whose sight I shall find favor." And she said to her, "Go, my daughter." So she set out and went and gleaned in the field after the reapers, and she happened to come to the part of the field belonging to Boaz, who was of the clan of Elimelech. And behold, Boaz came from Bethlehem. And he said to the reapers, "The LORD be with you!" And they answered, "The LORD bless you." Then Boaz said to his young man who was in charge of the reapers, "Whose young woman is this?" And the servant who was in charge of the reapers answered, "She is the young Moabite woman, who came back with Naomi from the country of Moab. She said, 'Please let me glean and gather among the sheaves after the reapers.' So she came, and she has continued from early morning until now, except for a short rest."

THE FIRST CHAPTER OF this book had focused on Naomi. This chapter begins by mentioning Naomi, but only so that the writer may introduce us to the next main character in the story: "Now Naomi had a relative of her husband's, a worthy man of the clan of Elimelech, whose name was Boaz." There is the name: Boaz. We do not run into him in person yet, but we are told his name. Naomi had painted a very bleak picture of her situation to any who would listen. In her own words, the Lord had "emptied" her. Her husband and her sons had died in Moab. Therefore, in her mind, there was no hope for her husband's genealogical line to continue. The line of Elimelech of the tribe of Judah would die with the deaths of Naomi and Ruth in Bethlehem, whenever that might be.

After hearing Ruth's confession, a reader of this story might expect that the two widows, Naomi and Ruth, would, in fact, return to Judah and Bethlehem and live out their days there until they both died, still unmarried and without children. Ruth said, "Do not urge me to leave you or to return from following you. For where you go I will go, and where you lodge I will lodge. Your people shall be my people, and your God my God. Where you die, I will die, and there will I be buried. May the Lord do so to me and more also if anything but death parts me from you" (1:16–17). Hearing these words at this point, we might pause, look forward in time and think that if Ruth follows her, this *is* what will happen. They will live in Bethlehem together, die together, and be buried there. Their graves then would be the final chapter of this story, which has turned out already to be sad and tragic. Not only would these two widows be buried together but their graves would also mark the end of Elimelech's line.

But with one sentence the writer infuses the reader with hope. Naomi was wrong. A potential redeemer would not have to come from her own womb. We would do well to remember that in her mind a child born to Naomi was the only way this family could be saved: "Turn back, my daughters; go your way, for I am too old to have a husband. If I should say I have hope, even if I should have a husband this night and should bear sons, would you therefore wait till they were grown? Would you therefore refrain from marrying?" (1:12–13). But our writer says, "No." There is a man, a blood relative of Naomi's former husband and therefore one who has the right to redeem this family through marriage. The writer gives us several characteristics of this man. First, his name is Boaz. Secondly, he is of the tribe of Elimelech, a fact mentioned two times in the first three verses. Thus, he is of the line of Judah. Judah was one of the twelve sons of Jacob. When Jacob blessed his sons at the end of Genesis, it was to Judah that the promise of a royal figure emerging from his bloodline was given (Gen 49:1, 8–12). We are told there that the hand of this son would remain on the neck of his enemies. His eyes would be darker than wine and his teeth whiter than milk. That promise seemed very distant, possibly even untrue, during this dark time in Israel when there was no king. But with the introduction

Chapter 1: An Introduction

to this new character, Boaz, there is perhaps a renewed hope, at the very least for Elimelech's line.

A third characteristic we are given in verse 1 related to this new character, Boaz of the line of Elimelech of Judah, is that he is a "worthy" man. This English phrase translates two words that mean something like "strong" and "valiant."[1] In other words, Boaz is a kind of hero, and thus worthy of respect. We will see more of what makes Boaz a *worthy* man as we go through this chapter. But for now, it might benefit us at this point to know that during the days when the judges ruled, one of the righteous judge-saviors of Israel, Gideon, is described in the same way. In the book of Judges, he is referred to as a "mighty man of valor" (6:12) which translates the two Hebrew words found here describing Boaz. The prophet Isaiah describes the character of the Messiah in this way: "For to us a child is born, to us a son is given; and the government shall be upon his shoulder, and his name shall be called Wonderful Counselor, Mighty God, Everlasting Father, Prince of Peace" (Isa 9:6). In these verses from Isaiah, "Mighty" translates one of the words used in this opening verse of chapter 2 regarding Boaz. The point that the writer wants us to see is that Boaz is a well-respected and strong man. This is a far cry from the other three men in their clan. Elimelech leads his family to Moab and dies there. His two sons are Mahlon and Chilion. As has already been observed, these names mean something like "weak" and "sickly." These sons, too, die in Moab. But Boaz is different. He is a "worthy" man. Could it be that Boaz will play a part in the destinies of Ruth and Naomi?

Boaz is referenced here in the text, and the very next verse mentions Ruth. Naomi is still in the picture, of course. In fact, Ruth speaks to her in verse 2 and Naomi responds, but Naomi's dominance in the story is beginning to fade. In chapter 1, Naomi leads the way from Moab back to Bethlehem. Ruth follows her. Once they get there, Naomi speaks to the women of the town, while Ruth is silent. But here, Ruth leads. She takes the initiative. She is a widowed foreigner in Israel. But she will not remain passive. She is active here, thinking already about how the two of them might provide for themselves. She says to Naomi, "Let me go to the field and glean among the ears of grain after him in whose sight I shall find favor" (Ruth 2:2). And Naomi responds, "Go, my daughter." Israelite law stated that the people of God were not to harvest grain right up to the edge of their fields in an effort to gather to themselves as much as possible. Rather, they were to leave

---

1. Block, *Judges, Ruth*, 651; Hubbard, *Book of Ruth*, 133; Holladay, *Concise*, 55, 102–3.

Part II: Ruth and Boaz

the outer edges and the leftovers for gleaning for the poor among them, including the sojourners and foreigners (Lev 19:9–10; 23:22; Deut 24:19). This was done to meet the needs of the hungry within their midst while also providing for themselves. It was a merciful act on the part of God's people, reflecting something of the mercy of their God, who continuously fed them.

Christians today still do this. The members of the church are not called to spend every dollar they make on themselves. There may be seasons when some in the church may have to do this, use most of their money, if not all, on themselves just to make ends meet. But overall, Christians are to *give*. They are to set aside a portion of their income to be freely given to the church. And a portion of what Christians give is used in precisely the same way as the outer edges of fields and the leftovers were used in Israel in Ruth's day. It is used to meet the needs of the poorest among the church's members, and even sometimes for the poor in the surrounding community.

This *portion* from the generosity of God's people is what Ruth was seeking. But this also meant that Ruth would have to work—and work hard. And this is what she did. We are told in verse 7 that she approached the supervisor of the fields and the reapers and requested permission to gather among the sheaves "after the reapers." Ruth, therefore, first had to request permission from Naomi to glean in the fields. Then, once she gets to the fields, she had to make a request of the supervisor of the reapers if she might be *allowed* to do this. After the permission was granted, she went out not just for an hour or two, but all day long. She did not sit at home bemoaning her situation, doing virtually nothing. She was active, fruitful, and submissive to authority. She sought to better herself and the life of her mother-in-law in whatever way she could. And because of *this*, she caught the eye of the owner of those fields, Boaz. Would Boaz have been as intrigued by her had he found out that she was doing nothing to help herself or her mother-in-law? We will never know, but it seems unlikely. Later in the story, Boaz tells Ruth, "All that you have done for your mother-in-law since the death of your husband has been fully told to me" (Ruth 2:11). Single women in the church who desire marriage would do well to take note of what was attractive to a worthy man like Boaz when he considered Ruth.

We are told here that Ruth, in the middle of her activity, steps right into the part of the field that belonged to Boaz: "So she set out and went and gleaned in the field after the reapers, and she happened to come to the part

Chapter 1: An Introduction

of the field belonging to Boaz" (v. 3). The writer plays with the reader somewhat here. He seems to imply with his wording that Ruth stepping into the field of Boaz happened by chance. It is as though the writer is saying fate brought Ruth to this part of the field. But the writer, under the inspiration of the Holy Spirit, knows there is no such thing as blind fate or chance. The dead idols of chance and fate, if believed and followed, make events in history part of an impersonal, random world-machine without purpose. The idea of fate also alleviates man from having to take responsibility for his actions. Was it according to fate that Mahlon and Chilion died after taking to themselves Moabite wives? Was it according to fate when an arrow struck the wicked King Ahab in battle when he was disguised as a regular soldier:?

> And the king of Israel said to Jehoshaphat, "I will disguise myself and go into battle, but you wear your robes." And the king of Israel disguised himself and went into battle. . . . But a certain man drew his bow at random and struck the king of Israel between the scale armor and the breastplate. . . . And the battle continued that day, and the king was propped up in his chariot facing the Syrians, until at evening he died. (1 Kgs 22:29–35)

In regard to Scripture's account of King Ahab's death, we are taught in verse 38 of the same chapter that the events leading up to the death of Ahab in battle, and even the details concerning his body and blood *after* his death, took place "according the word of the LORD that he had spoken" (v. 38). What we see in the extended passage from 1 Kings is that the writer playfully uses literary flourish, "at random," not to give credence to chance, but to further emphasize the sovereignty of God. The LORD God Almighty determines and governs all things, even to the human target and the puncture point of a seemingly random arrow. A similar literary device is being employed by the writer here in Ruth.[2] Fate had no hand in all of this. The god of chance does not exist. Elimelech, Mahlon, and Chilion died for a reason. Ruth walked into this portion of the field *according to the plan of God*. The writer uses this language of what seems to be happenstance to *accentuate* the exact opposite of what it appears to be teaching. In a playful, ironic way, the writer brings attention to this moment.[3] Ruth was being an

---

2. Hubbard, who agrees with this assessment, goes so far as to translate the portion of the verse in question in this way: "As luck would have it, she happened upon the piece of farmland belonging to Boaz." *Book of Ruth*, 140–41.

3. Block writes, "By excessively attributing Ruth's good fortune to chance, he forces the reader to sit up and take notice, to ask questions concerning the significance of everything that is transpiring. . . . In reality he is screaming, 'See the hand of God at work

obedient woman but God had purposed, from all eternity, that through her obedience she would walk right into the field of Boaz. Affirming God's absolute sovereignty, as it is clearly taught in the Bible, reminds us that *everything* happens for a reason. And it safeguards the truth that men are responsible to *this sovereign God* for their choices and actions.

So the writer lays emphasis upon God's holy providence in determining Ruth's steps. He then, in the very next verse, lays greater emphasis upon the physical arrival of the owner of this field: "And behold, Boaz" (Ruth 2:4). By inserting the word *behold* the writer is essentially saying, "Look, here he is! Boaz! Pay attention to him. Look here—here is where Naomi's and Ruth's lives have been headed all along, through all the heartbreak and suffering; Behold, Boaz!" And what do we learn of Boaz now that he is introduced to the reader in person? He is the owner of the harvest and he is the lord of the reapers. He is their master, and as their master he cares about them. He even prays for them and they respond with the same love and favor toward him: "And behold, Boaz came from Bethlehem. And he said to the reapers, 'The LORD be with you!' And they answered, 'The LORD bless you'" (v. 4). Part of the reason that Boaz is called a *worthy* man is found here: he enjoyed a mutual love and respect with those under his care. We are reminded of the words of Boaz's great grandson, King David, in regard to godly leadership: "When one rules justly over men, ruling in the fear of God, he dawns on them like the morning light, like the sun shining forth on a cloudless morning, like rain that makes grass to sprout from the earth" (1 Sam 23:3–4).

Next, we learn that Boaz noticed Ruth: "Then Boaz said to his young man who was in charge of the reapers, 'Whose young woman is this?'" (Ruth 2:5). This well-respected leader, Boaz, speaks to one of his superintendents, asking about a particular young woman in his field. Could it be that Ruth has achieved her goal stated in verse 2 in her request to Naomi? "Let me go to the field and glean among the ears of grain after him in whose sight I shall find favor." Will Boaz show *favor* to this one who has caught his eye? The superintendent tells Boaz what he knows about her. She is a Moabite who has come back from Moab with Naomi. And so, the writer brings the reader into contact with Boaz and we see already that he is asking about Ruth. But it is not yet revealed what the disposition of Boaz will be toward her. She had caught the eye of another man of Judah, Mahlon, several years

---

here!'" *Judges, Ruth*, 653.

Chapter 1: An Introduction

earlier. That did not end so well. What might take place between Ruth and this new character?

These questions will be answered in due time, but for now what can be learned from this section? The writer has left us with an image of Boaz looking out over his fields and taking notice of one woman. It is obvious she is in some way set apart from the others, at least in his own eyes. Boaz likely knew his servants and therefore he would have recognized Ruth was not one of them. She was doing her work *after* the reapers. But we would do well to notice that Ruth is closely associated with the harvest itself. In verse 2 she asks Naomi if she may glean among the ears of grain. Then in verse 3, we are told that she "set out and went and gleaned in the field after the reapers." Additionally, her request to the supervisor is repeated: "She said, 'Please let me glean and gather among the sheaves after the reapers" (v. 7). So, Ruth is gleaning in the midst of fields ripe for harvesting when Boaz notices her. Is this fact significant?

In the New Testament, believers are represented as a harvest field and Jesus is Lord of the harvest (Matt 3:12; 9:36–38; 13:30; Luke 10:1–2; 1 Cor 15:23, 42–44). At the resurrection, believers will all be gathered up. But the church is also represented in Scripture as the bride of Christ (Matt 9:15; John 2:1–11; Eph 5:25–32; Rev 19:6–8). This is what Ruth is to Boaz (though he did not know it at this point). She is his bride-to-be among the golden harvest fields. The two Biblical symbols of the church converge somewhat here. He takes notice of her, *only* her. We will see that he gives his singular love to her in becoming her husband. And the LORD accomplishes all of this. He brought Ruth to Boaz. Before this happened, God raised up Boaz to the status of worthy so that he would be able to receive his bride. Boaz is the new Elimelech for this family, a *better* one. Therefore, through Boaz, God will raise this family line from the dead just as he raises seed sown in the ground into a full and glorious harvest.

For the believer, we would benefit greatly to understand and appreciate that this is what all of the world's history is about. Every death, every life, every encounter and event (even those events that appear to happen by chance), *everything* occurs so that every one of God's elect will walk into the field of their Redeemer and meet their true husband Jesus Christ, raised from the dead. One day we will see Jesus, the greater Boaz, and like the writer says here, the whole church will sing praises to him, saying "Behold, Jesus!"

Part II: Ruth and Boaz

Ruth, Naomi, and Boaz will do the same on that day, but for now, in this part of our story, Boaz has only taken an initial interest in Ruth. Will this interest grow into something more? Will he talk to her? This all remains to be seen.

Chapter 2: Conversation

RUTH 2:8–13

Then Boaz said to Ruth, "Now, listen, my daughter, do not go to glean in another field or leave this one, but keep close to my young women. Let your eyes be on the field that they are reaping, and go after them. Have I not charged the young men not to touch you? And when you are thirsty, go to the vessels and drink what the young men have drawn." Then she fell on her face, bowing to the ground, and said to him, "Why have I found favor in your eyes, that you should take notice of me, since I am a foreigner?" But Boaz answered her, "All that you have done for your mother-in-law since the death of your husband has been fully told to me, and how you left your father and mother and your native land and came to a people that you did not know before. The Lord repay you for what you have done, and a full reward be given you by the Lord, the God of Israel, under whose wings you have come to take refuge!" Then she said, "I have found favor in your eyes, my lord, for you have comforted me and spoken kindly to your servant, though I am not one of your servants."

This section begins with Boaz and Ruth in conversation. If we consider this book in terms of a romantic story, this is the moment where the two lovers meet for the first time. It begins with Boaz speaking to Ruth: "Now, listen, my daughter." We can stop here for a moment because in verse 1 the writer refers to Boaz as a *worthy* man. What makes him worthy or

Part II: Ruth and Boaz

honorable? What kind of man should a Christian woman, desiring to be married, be looking for? What kind of man should fathers and mothers of Christian daughters hope for as a son-in-law? Certainly, they would want to find a *worthy* man. On the other side of this, what kind of men are Christian men supposed to be, whether married or single? They are to be *worthy* men. We learn something of what this means and what it looks like in Boaz.

Boaz is an Israelite at home in Judah. He is called a *worthy* man; therefore, he is honored among the people of Israel. We have already seen that his workers spoke well of him (Ruth 2:4). We learn that he owns fields and has servants and laborers. He also has enough resources to provide for Ruth and Naomi. Ruth, however, is from Moab, a pagan nation, generally despised by Israelites and considered to be a nation of unclean people. Later in the story, we meet another Israelite redeemer who had the right to marry Ruth and redeem this family *ahead* of Boaz. But he turns down the opportunity. More precisely, as will be shown in a subsequent chapter, he refuses to accept the obligation. He chooses to do this because he thinks that association with this Moabite woman would tarnish his name and inheritance: "I cannot redeem . . . lest I impair my own inheritance" (4:6). To the other man of Judah, Ruth was considered to be inferior.

In addition, Ruth is a widow and she is poor. Providing food for herself and her mother-in-law meant that she had to glean the leftovers in someone else's field and harvest. This would happen *only* if the person who owned the field was merciful and allowed her to do so. If we compare the two here, Ruth and Boaz, one might expect Boaz to immediately assert his superiority over Ruth. Or perhaps he may choose not to even speak face-to-face with her. Since he is such a worthy man, maybe Boaz should have a representative of his go speak to Ruth on his behalf until Ruth can prove to him that she is worthy to be in his presence. This is not what Boaz does because this is not part of the essence of Biblical manhood. Thus, we are taught here what it means to be a *worthy* man. Consider what Boaz does. He speaks to Ruth face-to-face and refers to her as his daughter: "Now, listen, my daughter." He regards Ruth as a virtual equal, another honored family member among the people of God in Israel.[1] With this initial greeting, he affirms her dignity and he gives rightful honor to her as a woman in Judah among a people in covenant with God.

He also displays his gentleness with her here. He will show more of this later. Ruth is vulnerable. She is under the threat of attack by less worthy

---

1. Block, *Judges, Ruth*, 659.

Chapter 2: Conversation

men. Boaz told the men not to touch her: "Let your eyes be on the field that they are reaping, and go after them. Have I not charged the young men not to touch you?" (2:9). Later, Naomi tells Ruth to do what Boaz says: "It is good, my daughter, that you go out with his young women, lest in another field you be assaulted" (v. 22). And now, here comes a man who has the authority and the resources to take advantage of a woman like Ruth. But he does not do so. He is overwhelmingly gentle with her.

His reference to her as *my daughter* is immediately followed with assuring words that he is deeply concerned about her well-being and will do everything in his power to protect her: "Do not glean in another field or leave this one, but keep close to my young women." Boaz also makes it clear to his men that they, too, are to treat Ruth as an equal. In the ancient Near East, water was usually drawn from wells, which took significant effort. One might think that Ruth, being a foreigner *and* a woman, should draw water *for* the men of Boaz. But Boaz turns this expectation around. Boaz will serve Ruth and so will his men: "Let your eyes be on the field they are reaping, and go after them. Have I not charged the young men not to touch you? And when you are thirsty, go to the vessels and drink what the young men have drawn" (v. 9).[2]

And what is Ruth's response to Boaz's kindness? She is not proud nor resentful. Ruth responds to the gentle love of Boaz with willing submissiveness and humility: "Then she fell on her face, bowing to the ground, and said to him, 'Why have I found favor in your eyes, that you should take notice of me, since I am a foreigner?'" (v. 10). Ruth displays recognition that she is undeserving of such mercy. We are reminded of the way in which another gentile woman in the Bible displayed a similar character. There was a Canaanite woman whose daughter was oppressed by a demon. She approached Jesus looking for mercy, that she might find favor in his eyes. Jesus said to her, "I was sent only to the lost sheep of the house of Israel. . . . It is not right to take the children's bread and throw it to the dogs" (Matt 15:24–26). And she said, "Yes, Lord, yet even the dogs eat the crumbs that fall from their master's table." Then Jesus responded, "O woman, great is your faith! Be it done for you as you desire," and her daughter was healed instantly. Jesus emphasized the Jewish/gentile distinction at the time, not to humiliate the gentile woman from Canaan, but to honor the

---

2. Block writes, "In a cultural context in which normally foreigners would draw for Israelites, and women would draw for men (Gen 24:10–20), Boaz's authorization of Ruth to drink from water his men had drawn is indeed extraordinary." *Judges, Ruth*, 660.

redemptive-historical moment. He had not yet gone to the cross where the dividing wall separating these two groups would forever be broken down. And yet this interaction provided an occasion to highlight this gentile's profound faith and deep humility. Characteristics like this were, for the most part at this time, not to be found among Christ's own people, the Jews. And so, it was the Jews, in the end, that were humiliated in this context. *They, and not the Canaanite woman, should* have had faith like hers.

We see then that Ruth's request (prayer?) was granted: "Let me go to the field and glean among the ears of grain after him in whose eyes I have found favor" (Ruth 2:2). Here she says to Boaz, "Why have I found favor in your eyes?" and again "I have found favor in your eyes" (vv. 10, 13). Thus, in Boaz, God gave Ruth what she was looking for and she responds to Boaz favorably: "You have comforted me and spoken kindly to your servant" (v. 13). What honest woman would not respond favorably and joyfully, with a submissive spirit, to a man such as this?

Boaz is sincere, kind, affirming, and gentle. He wants to protect her, and to do so he is willing to place himself between Ruth and his men, telling them not to touch her. More than this, he seeks to ensure that she will be treated as an equal among the other workers. She would drink the same water the others drank. The very water that the men drew was to be shared with her. Ruth affirms Boaz's kindness with what she said about him in verse 13: "I have found favor in your eyes, my lord, for you have comforted me and spoken kindly to your servant." She even refers to him as her *lord*. We also see that Boaz prays for Ruth: "The LORD repay you for what you have done, and a full reward be given you by the LORD, the God of Israel, under whose wings you have come to take refuge!" (v. 12). Boaz also had to work very hard before he even met Ruth so that he could be in a position to care for her in this way. This is what is expected from the men of the church, the fellow worthy men who follow Christ by faith. Boaz, by God's grace, was able to balance the hardness, firmness, and manly strength that are required in the fields with the gentleness, kindness, and graciousness that are needed to personally care for a woman. If a Christian man desires to win over a woman (even if that woman may already be his wife) in an unselfish and God-honoring way, this is how it is done. He is to have manly strength in the fields and gentleness at home. To put this another way, winning the honor and respect of a woman is *not* properly done by attempting to assert dominance over her or treating her as an inferior. This is so because, essentially, she is *not* an inferior. In God's eyes she has exactly equal rights to

Chapter 2: Conversation

the kingdom of Christ as the man does. God regards the man *in Christ*. And God regards the woman *in Christ*. If this is how God regards our sisters in the church, the men in the church are to do the same. *In Christ*, she is a joint heir of the kingdom, a fellow laborer for Christ's church, and a partner in the gospel (Rom 8:16-17; 16:1-2; Phil 1:4; 4:2-3).

It is not to be doubted that Boaz was *physically* attracted to Ruth. There is nothing inherently wrong with having a strong physical attraction toward a person of the opposite sex, especially if that person is one's spouse. One only has to think of the Song of Solomon and the way in which the king and queen in this book speak delightfully of one another's very pleasing physical attributes. There is also nothing inherently wrong with seeking to make ourselves as physically attractive as possible. This might be done to possibly attract a marriage partner, if the person is single, or if the person is married, this might be done to look good for one's spouse. However, this is not all there is to marriage. Boaz says to Ruth, "All that you have done for your mother-in-law since the death of your husband has been fully told me, and how you left your father and mother and your native land and came to a people that you did not know before" (Ruth 2:11). Boaz was attracted to her godly character, her courage, her faith and perseverance, and her self-denial. Ruth is described here as being much like Abraham, the father of the Israelite nation. Abraham left his native country and journeyed to a land he did not know before. Where was faith like this in Israel at this time of the rule of the judges? It was rare indeed. And yet here we are given Abraham-like faith from a *Moabite* widow.

As Boaz praises Ruth for her faithfulness and kindness to Naomi, he uses one of the most tender and comforting Biblical images of God's love and care of his people.[3] And he uses it to sum up in one phrase Ruth's journey to Bethlehem and her continued obedience in Bethlehem. Boaz says that in doing these things, Ruth has "taken refuge under the wings of the God of Israel" (v. 12). This image is used in places throughout the Old Testament (Deut 32:11; Isa 31:5; Ps 57:1; 91:4). Jesus used this image in referring to Jerusalem's refusal to take refuge in him (Matt 23:37). In this illustration, God is depicted as a mother bird that stretches her wings out over her defenseless young, shielding them from would-be predators and from the heat of the sun. In this way the mother bird protects them and guards them. While the imagery is presented somewhat differently in various places, the context of each clearly teaches that it refers to God's

---

3. Block, *Judges, Ruth*, 663-64.

intimate, loving care and protection of his covenant people.[4] In following Naomi and taking up residence in Bethlehem, this is what Ruth had done; she had taken refuge under the wings of the God of Israel.

In reality, Boaz is saying more than he actually knows. Ruth is in Judah and is working in the fields of Boaz. She had already taken refuge under the shadow of the Lord's wings. The God of Israel was already caring for her and protecting her. But we see also that Boaz was *becoming*, and *would become* in an even fuller way, the very wings of God for Ruth. In marriage, Boaz would spread his wings over Ruth, and in *this* way, God would further care for and protect this young woman from Moab.

For believers, this is what Jesus has done for us. In covenant, he spreads his wings over us. We, by faith, as weak, vulnerable people—former *spiritual* widows and orphans—find *permanent* refuge under his care. How does Jesus do this? He displays infinite strength in the fields by going to the cross to die for us. He referred to his suffering and dying as his *work* (John 17:4). Bearing the wrath of God against our sin is something no other man could do. Jesus did this *for us*. Every day that Christ woke up on this earth was a day lived in progress toward death on a cross as a substitute for his people. But then Jesus also comes *to us*. We come face-to-face with Jesus in the hearing of the gospel. And what does he do? He comforts us. He speaks kindly to us. He refers to us as his sons and daughters. He assures us that our enemies cannot ultimately harm us. He is gentle with us because we are incredibly vulnerable creatures. And in all of this, we recognize that we are undeserving of such grace from God: "Why have I found favor in your eyes, that you should take notice of me" (Ruth 2:10). What should our response be to such love? We joyfully and willingly submit to his lordship. Like Ruth, we bow our faces to the ground and say, "Thank you, God, for showing me, an undeserving sinner and foreigner to your love, such mercy; I am your servant."

At this point in the story, Boaz and Ruth have only just met. The conversation went well. Should Boaz now ask Ruth out on a date? We find out in the next section that they do share a meal together. Let us turn there now.

---

4. Walton et al., *Old Testament*, 205–6; 521.

Chapter 3: Dining Together

RUTH 2:14-16

And at mealtime Boaz said to her, "Come here and eat some bread and dip your morsel in the wine." So she sat beside the reapers, and he passed to her roasted grain. And she ate until she was satisfied, and she had some left over. When she rose to glean, Boaz instructed his young men, saying, "Let her glean even among the sheaves, and do not reproach her. And also pull out some from the bundles for her and leave it for her to glean, and do not rebuke her."

From where we left off, the scene shifts to the midday meal. In verse 17, it shifts again to Ruth finishing out the day and working until evening, then having a discussion about Boaz. So, we can follow the text and think about this meal scene by itself. We have just seen Boaz extend compassion, generosity, and love toward Ruth in their first encounter. Ruth responds with thankful submission and humility. We were left with Ruth saying this: "I have found favor in your eyes, my lord, for you have comforted me and spoken kindly to your servant, though I am not one of your servants" (v. 13). Ruth is full of thanksgiving that she, a foreigner and a widow, has received such grace from this man and from the Lord God of Israel. She also affirms in this statement to Boaz that she is his servant and that she is more than willing to serve him. And yet, right after this we see Boaz *serving Ruth* at a meal: "At mealtime Boaz said to her, 'Come here and eat some bread and dip your morsel in the wine.' So she sat beside the reapers, and he passed to her roasted grain" (v. 14). We are given further insight into Boaz's character. He is a *worthy* man. As a worthy man he is not above sharing a meal with his servants and workers. He then invites Ruth to enjoy a more intimate fellowship in the meal by coming closer to the group. He says to her, "Come here." This request will be looked at in more detail shortly, but for now we can appreciate the way in which the writer isolates this scene. It centers upon the meal. It focuses on the actions taken and the words spoken during this midday dinner.

We would do well at this point to think about meals in general. Meals are not simply a means by which we get energy for work and life, though that is part of the reason we break bread. Some of our meals are eaten alone. Some of our meals are quickly eaten because of a need to be somewhere at a certain time. These are not inherently bad ways to eat at times. But meals are not *just* for the food. They are not like putting fuel in a car. People do not have personal relationships with automobiles. Stopping for gasoline does not include having table fellowship with one's vehicle. Meals with other people, like all things really, are *theological*. What we see in God's word is that something significant takes place when individuals and families sit down or recline to share a meal together.[1]

In the beginning, God prepared a feast for Adam and Eve in the garden. Out of the ground God made to spring up every tree that was pleasant to the sight and good for food. He said to the first man, Adam: "You may surely eat of every tree of the garden, but of the tree of the knowledge of good and evil you shall not eat, for in the day that you eat of it you shall surely die" (Gen 2:16–17). Then God said that it was not good for man to be alone. So, for Adam and *from* Adam, he made Eve, Adam's wife. God did this by taking one of Adam's ribs and forming it into a woman, and he brought that woman to the man. Therefore, in covenant with one another in marriage and in covenant with God, Adam and Eve were to enjoy meals *together*. If at this point we still do not think shared meals are all that important, we would do well to think about what happened next. Adam brought sin and death into the world through improper *eating!* (Gen 3:1–19). Adam disobeyed God and *ate* from the prohibited tree. There is meaning and purpose in sharing meals together.

In considering further scriptural teaching on this matter, we will remember that Abraham showed hospitality *to the* LORD, by way of a meal, when the LORD appeared to Abraham in Gen 18. There we learn that Abraham saw three men standing in front of him near the door of his tent. So, he

---

1. Block, *Judges, Ruth*, 666.

Chapter 3: Dining Together

had Sarah begin making a meal for them while Abraham himself prepared a calf. It was at this meal that the Lord announced to Abraham and his wife that within a year they would have a son (Gen 18:1–10). We are told in Psalm 23 that the Lord prepares *a table* before us in the presence of our enemies. In Jesus's parable about the prodigal son, the father in the parable prepares a great feast to celebrate and be glad that his son, "though once dead, was alive," and "he was lost but was found" (Luke 15:11–32). There is meaning and purpose in sharing meals together, just as there is meaning and purpose in the meal spoken of here in Ruth, which is why the writer highlights this moment.

At this point, the writer has not given his hearers any explicit suggestion that Boaz and Ruth are romantically interested in one another. Ruth does not know yet that Boaz is a redeemer. Nevertheless, a bond is being forged here. Boaz says to Ruth, "Come here." Prior to these words, Ruth, as a Moabite, may have positioned herself in such a way to communicate her appreciation that close involvement with Israelites was not the socially accepted practice.[2] So, she kept her distance. She was, after all, an outsider—a non-Israelite. But Boaz does not want any such distinction to be made here. And he wants the others around him to know this. So, he invites her to take bread from the very hands of the master of the fields, dip it in wine, and eat. And she was to do this while sitting right next to his other servants, *among* them. Taken all together, at this point in time, this was the closest possible fellowship conceivable that this young Moabite woman could enjoy with this group of Israelites. It was one thing to let her glean behind the reapers. And maybe they would even be able to understand allowing Ruth to drink the water that was drawn up by the men. But sitting right next to her at a meal and watching her take bread from Boaz—who had obviously taken notice of her—this may have been too much for a prideful Israelite to accept.

We may think of the apostle Peter here. Peter had been rebuked by the apostle Paul for discriminatory thinking, such as might have been present at this meal in Ruth had not Boaz taken the lead. Peter had been eating with gentiles when he saw members of the Jewish circumcision party approaching. Upon seeing this, he separated himself from the gentiles. What was Peter's motive in doing this? He did this because eating a meal with gentiles represented and signified close fellowship, a bond even, with uncircumcised people. The members of this party rejected having this type of

---

2. Block, *Judges, Ruth*, 666.

Part II: Ruth and Boaz

communion with non-Jews, and had they seen Peter eating with them they would have certainly rebuked him or even condemned his actions. Peter separated himself from the meal with the gentiles to avoid such persecution.

Boaz, however, would not take part in any action that would communicate to Ruth and the others that she should be excluded from this group. The message is very clear: Ruth belongs at this table. This truth is confirmed, on some level, by this meal. Thus, Ruth dines with Boaz. We are told that she ate, and that she was satisfied and had some left over. We can think back on Psalm 23 here: "You prepare a table before me in the presence of my enemies . . . my cup overflows." Ruth was filled and had more left over. This is what our Redeemer does for us. He fills us to overflowing. Our cup runs over.

Presently, we may consider the state of this family prior to arriving in Bethlehem. They had been emptied by the LORD. But now, through Boaz, the LORD begins to fill them again. The Bible consistently reminds us that God fills the hungry with good things (Ps 107:9; 145:16; 146:7; Matt 6:25–26). Jesus fed five thousand hungry people on one occasion and then, later, another four thousand (Matt 14:13–21; 15:32–39). In each instance we are told that after everyone was satisfied, there was food left over. It should not be a surprise then that God was filling this family in Bethlehem. The refilling of Ruth and Naomi by the LORD was in keeping with his character as the God who is abounding in steadfast love and faithfulness.

Ruth had eaten and was satisfied. After the meal Ruth gets up to head back to work. Boaz is not silent. This is an incredible thing here that he does. In front of all his servants and reapers, Boaz says this: "Let her glean even among the sheaves, and do not reproach her. And also pull out some from the bundles for her and leave it for her to glean, and do not rebuke her" (Ruth 2:15–16). Boaz is the leader and captain of this organization. As leader, he authoritatively gives two commands and they are both about Ruth. Ruth, this young Moabite widow, is to have full and free access to the harvest of Boaz. Twice he says "let her glean." Twice also in these verses he gives commands in regard to Ruth's physical and emotional safety: "Do not reproach her. . . . Do not rebuke her." If there was anything left in Ruth that made her think she did not belong in Bethlehem, it should have all but evaporated after this meal. By his sovereign word as leader, by welcoming her to his table, by feeding Ruth, filling her with his bread and wine, satisfying her to the point that she had more left over, by granting her free access to the harvest field, and by commanding that she be protected from

Chapter 3: Dining Together

evil of any kind, Boaz made it clear, at least in his own mind, that Ruth had been grafted into the life and fellowship of Israel. In a word, Boaz made it abundantly clear that Ruth *belonged* there, with him, with this family, the family of Elimelech, and with his other servants. She belonged.[3] And the others were to treat her as such.

For the Christian, this is what our Leader, and Captain of the Harvest, does for us. For those who come to him by faith, Jesus invites us to come close to him. He welcomes us to his table. He gives us his body and his blood as true food and true drink. By speaking his sovereign word over us, he assures us that we have been grafted into his body. Though we were once gentiles and outcasts, cut off from the covenant blessings of God, as Ruth had been, by the blood of Jesus we have been brought *near* to God. We belong with him and we belong in close table fellowship with his people. We have been grafted into the vine of Israel. We belong to and are an organic part of the same body of which Boaz, Ruth, Naomi, David, Isaiah, Elijah, Abraham, Sarah, Isaac, Rebekah, Jacob, and Rachel, among many other Old Testament saints, are a part. This is who we are as Christians—the body of Christ. In fellowship with the members of his body is where we belong. This is not all there is, however. Jesus, by his word, assures us that the evil one cannot ultimately harm us. We may suffer, we may be harassed, we may even die for the sake of Christ, but ultimately *nothing* can snatch us from the hands of our Redeemer. Jesus, thus, in regard to our eternal safety, says to Satan and his minions: "do not reproach her."

Finally, this meal between Ruth and Boaz and the other servants gives us a picture of what takes place at the Lord's Supper in the new covenant. In the Lord's Supper, through the partaking of bread and wine, our Redeemer, Jesus, gives us his body and his blood. He extends his hand to us at this meal in order to spiritually satisfy us, fill us up to overflowing, so that we might have strength to glean in the harvest fields. In this holy meal, we have our union and fellowship with Jesus and his people confirmed, solidified and sealed in our hearts, just as Boaz confirmed Ruth's communion with Israel at this midday supper while briefly resting from the labors of the day.

---

3. Hubbard writes, "She became a virtual member of Boaz's entourage . . . the permission, provision, and protection that Boaz gave Ruth (vv. 8–9, 15–16; cf. v. 22) certainly signaled his sponsorship of her. The meal scene confirmed this relation, for there Boaz not only welcomed Ruth to sit beside his workers but also himself served her food." *Book of Ruth*, 193–94.

Part II: Ruth and Boaz

Ruth goes back to work, but that evening she had quite a lot to talk about with her mother-in-law. In the next chapter we will see how Naomi reacts to the news of Ruth's encounter with Boaz.

Chapter 4: Telling Naomi

RUTH 2:17-23

So she gleaned in the field until evening. Then she beat out what she had gleaned, and it was about an ephah of barley. And she took it up and went into the city. Her mother-in-law saw what she had gleaned. She also brought out and gave her what food she had left over after being satisfied. And her mother-in-law said to her, "Where did you glean today? And where have you worked? Blessed be the man who took notice of you." So she told her mother-in-law with whom she had worked and said, "The man's name with whom I worked today is Boaz." And Naomi said to her daughter-in-law, "May he be blessed by the Lord, whose kindness has not forsaken the living or the dead!" Naomi also said to her, "The man is a close relative of ours, one of our redeemers." And Ruth the Moabite said, "Besides, he said to me, 'You shall keep close by my young men until they have finished all my harvest.'" And Naomi said to Ruth, her daughter-in-law, "It is good, my daughter, that you go out with his young women, lest in another field you be assaulted." So she kept close to the young women of Boaz, gleaning until the end of the barley and wheat harvests. And she lived with her mother-in-law.

Ruth and Boaz had shared a meal together at lunchtime, though they were not alone. We are told that she was fully satisfied by the food she ate and that she had some left over. After this, we are told in verse 17 that Ruth

Part II: Ruth and Boaz

"gleaned in the field until evening." So, this young girl remains active. She accepted the invitation from Boaz to dine with him and the other workers. Now it is time to go back to work. Ruth is a widow. She is a foreigner and she is poor. But she does not use her situation as an excuse to be lazy or inactive. She does not complain. She gets to work. She contributes, working hard in this desperate and sad time to help support herself and her mother-in-law, who is also a widow.

We would do well to notice what Ruth does when she returns home from the fields. She gives Naomi food, and she also gives her some of the leftovers from lunchtime.[1] Ruth is working for herself *and* for her mother-in-law: "She took it up and went into the city. Her mother-in-law saw what she had gleaned. She also brought out and gave her what food she had left over after being satisfied" (v. 18). Ruth is going out into the fields away from the city to work: "Where did you glean today? And where have you worked?" (v. 19). She is doing this not for herself alone, but to meet the needs of Naomi as well. We must also remember here that the fields in which she works belong to Boaz. Ultimately, the abundance of food is coming from, not just any fields, but the fields *of Boaz*. But grain will not magically appear in Ruth and Naomi's house. And Boaz, the business man, certainly did not get to the financial position in which he was at this time by giving handouts. It was apparent he was generous, but he also had to be wise. If this abundance in Boaz's fields was to be actually enjoyed by this family, Ruth was required to be active and work, to serve. She had to deny herself and glean for her sake and for the sake of her mother-in-law.

This next observation can go unnoticed as one reads this story, but consider how much grain Ruth produced from gleaning: "So she gleaned in the field until evening. Then she beat out what she had gleaned, and it was about an ephah of barley" (v. 17). An ephah was approximately twenty-two liters of grain.[2] In a modern context, we might imagine a one-liter soda bottle filled instead with grain and barley (i.e., cereal). Multiply this by twenty-two and we have something close to what Ruth produced, *in one day!* This ephah of barley would have weighed between thirty and fifty pounds.[3] It is amazing how the Lord can bless our productivity if we are faithful, obediently working hard while continuously having the needs of

---

1. Hubbard, *Book of Ruth*, 181; see also 181n7 pointing out a chiastic structure in this part of verse 18 coupled with the initial reference to what was left over in verse 14.
2. Hubbard, *Book of Ruth*, 179; Block, *Judges, Ruth*, 670.
3. Hubbard, *Book of Ruth*, 179; Block, *Judges, Ruth*, 670.

Chapter 4: Telling Naomi

others on our minds in addition to our own. This is what Ruth was doing here. This is the abundant productivity of one woman in one day (and with a lunch break at that). One can only speculate what an Israelite *man* might have produced in one day under the same circumstances. There is, then, a lesson here about what is expected of women in the community of the faithful. We may consider the activities of the ideal God-fearing woman that are listed in chapter 31 of Proverbs. The woman described here is an "excellent wife" (Prov 31:10). What makes her excellent? She "seeks wool and flax, and works with willing hands" (v. 13). She buys real estate (v. 16). She rises early to care for her family and even stays up at night to finish her work (vv. 15, 18). She "makes linen garments and sells them" (v. 24). Ruth is single at this point and young. She does not have young babies at home (yet!) and her role probably changed somewhat once she marries Boaz who is able to provide for her. But we can be certain that Ruth remained active as the wife of Boaz, serving him and the family with hard work. The attributes of the "excellent" woman of Proverbs are evident in Ruth already. And of course, if we fast-forward to the end, the fruit that ultimately resulted from Ruth's excellent productivity in Boaz's home was nothing less than a king (Ruth 4:17).

Not every woman's activity in the church and at home will look exactly like the activity of the sister next to them. One woman may homeschool her children, while another sends her children to school. One woman may be a full-time homemaker, while another goes out to the fields to work, as did Ruth. We should not leave out the many activities and tasks accomplished by women in service of the church. Whatever it is that women in Christ's church are called to do, they are to be faithful. They are to continue to walk in obedience. In addition to their own needs, they are to have the needs of others on their minds. The mature women in the church are to set an example for the younger ones in their congregations as to what it looks like to be a woman such as Ruth in a modern context. We see here, then, that Ruth the Moabite gives the women in the church, of any generation, an example to follow.

The amount of barley Ruth brings home causes Naomi to question her as to where in the world she was able to gather so much: "Where did you glean today? And where have you worked?" (2:19). We should remember that it was *to Boaz* that these women were headed all along. When we first met Boaz in this chapter, the writer fronted his name in order to bring attention to the man: "And behold, Boaz" (v. 4). Here the writer brings

Part II: Ruth and Boaz

attention to him again, but in a different way. Instead of fronting Boaz's name, we find it at the end of Ruth's response to Naomi: "So she told her mother-in-law with whom she had worked and said, 'The man's name with whom I worked today is Boaz'"[4] (v. 19). This is the first and only time in this story that the name of Boaz is put on the lips of Ruth. The writer mentioned him at the beginning of this chapter, but at that point in the story, Naomi had not remembered him and Ruth had yet to meet him. Now, however, Ruth is saying his name—*Boaz*.

The mention of *that* name immediately causes another response from Naomi. For reasons unknown to us, in the midst of their sadness Naomi had forgotten about Boaz. Perhaps the Lord blocked Boaz out of her mind so that he might bring glory to himself in this way. Or maybe it was Naomi's extreme bitterness that clouded her memory. Whatever the reason, she remembers immediately, at this point, who this man is. The mention of his name elicits a shout of praise from Naomi. She declares to Ruth who he is and what he means to this family. Boaz is a redeemer, a gō'ēl (v. 20).[5] As a *redeemer* Boaz was a close relative, a blood relative of Naomi's. Therefore, he had the right and the privilege to redeem this family from the darkness and sadness in which they lived.

To redeem means to reclaim or buy back. In this context, Boaz, as a "close relative," had the legal right, according to Israelite law, to reclaim Elimelech's line from childlessness. If Boaz were to marry Ruth, they could have children together and the name of Elimelech of Judah would continue. For Naomi, this name, Boaz, had just put a shot of hope in this family. With the arrival of Boaz, a ray of light has shown in their darkness. Where once the words of her mouth were filled with bitterness, now Naomi praises the Lord. Hope for the future has come into this home.

Like any good mother whose daughter meets a fine young man like Boaz, Naomi begins to plan how she might permanently get these two together. In verse 22, Naomi tells Ruth to stay close to the female workers of Boaz. Naomi, the matchmaker, will go even further with her plans in the next chapter. But for now, this dialogue between Ruth and Naomi reminds us of the power of the name of Jesus. For those who believe, the name of Jesus gives us hope, *real* hope and *real* joy. There is power in his name. Jesus

---

4. Block, *Judges, Ruth*, 671. Block gives additional comments in regard to the literary devices used here to further dramatize the announcement of Boaz. So also Hubbard, *Book of Ruth*, 184–85.

5. Hubbard, *Book of Ruth*, 188–89; Block, *Judges, Ruth*, 674–78.

Chapter 4: Telling Naomi

is our gō'ēl, our Redeemer. With the price of his life, he buys us back from darkness. When we were empty, by giving us faith to believe on that name, God fills us again and he secures our future. Because of that name, Jesus, no matter what may befall us in this life, we always have something for which to look forward—resurrection glory.

The writer is really attempting to drive his readers crazy here however. Even with Ruth saying Boaz's name and Naomi giving a shout of praise and starting to plan Ruth's wedding, we still do not really know what will happen.[6] The chapter ends with this: "So she kept close to the young women of Boaz, gleaning until the end of the barley and wheat harvests. And she lived with her mother-in-law" (v. 23). Though real possibilities have opened up with the introduction of Boaz into their story, there is no significant change yet in the lives of these women.[7] Ruth continues to work and she continues to live with Naomi. How long will things stay this way? Could there be a roadblock around the corner that would permanently keep these two from coming together? We must turn to part three in order to find out.

---

6. Hubbard, *Book of Ruth*, 189.
7. Hubbard, *Book of Ruth*, 193.

Part III: The Threshing Floor

Chapter 1: Initiation of the Plan

RUTH 3:1–5

Then Naomi her mother-in-law said to her, "My daughter, should I not seek rest for you, that it may be well with you? Is not Boaz our relative, with whose young women you were? See, he is winnowing barley tonight at the threshing floor. Wash therefore and anoint yourself, and put on your cloak and go down to the threshing floor, but do not make yourself known to the man until he has finished eating and drinking. But when he lies down, observe the place where he lies. Then go and uncover his feet and lie down, and he will tell you what to do." And she replied, "All that you say I will do."

It seems as though some time has passed since we last heard Naomi and Ruth discussing Boaz.[1] We are told in verse 23 of the previous chapter that Ruth kept close to the young women of Boaz, gleaning until the end of the barley and wheat harvests. After the harvesting, the grain would have to be collected and gathered onto the threshing floor, which would have likely taken days, or even weeks. From Naomi's perspective, the relationship between Boaz and Ruth, at this point, may not be moving along as fast as she would have liked.[2] It seems that neither Boaz nor Ruth have taken any kind of initiative to move the relationship forward. So, like any good mother-in-law who sees a good thing possibly happening before her,

---

1. Block, *Judges, Ruth*, 679.
2. Block writes, "Obviously he was not making any moves; so as Ruth's mother-in-law, Naomi took it upon herself to overcome his inertia." *Judges, Ruth*, 680.

she starts to think how she herself might help this relationship get off the ground. Perhaps, also, she is starting to see visions of grandchildren when once there were none, and when there was no hope even for such a thing. Naomi is not about to let this opportunity slip away. So, she begins to speak to her daughter-in-law, Ruth.

This section is almost entirely made up of Naomi's words to Ruth.[3] In English, there are only seven words from Ruth in these five verses: "All that you say I will do" (v. 5). In Hebrew, there are only four. This domination of the dialogue by Naomi reminds us of the beginning of this story. For the most part, Naomi monopolized the speaking. But those speeches had a different flavor then. They were filled with bitterness and somewhat of a hopelessness. For example, let us consider what she said to her sisters in Israel at the beginning of barley harvest: "Do not call me Naomi; call me 'Mara,' for the Almighty has dealt very bitterly with me. I went away full and the LORD has brought me back empty. Why call me Naomi, when the LORD has testified against me and the Almighty has brought calamity upon me?" (1:20–21). She has changed since then. As previously mentioned, Naomi means "pleasant." This is what she is becoming again. It is "pleasant" to hear her voice now. Why? Her overall spirit has changed because she is now filled with hope. Her future and the future of her family have opened up with new possibilities. We could recall the time when Naomi wanted to rid herself of Ruth. At one point, she repeatedly told her daughter-in-law Ruth to "turn back" and "go back" to Moab. Ruth, of course, refused. Consider the first thing Naomi says to Ruth here, however: "My daughter, should I not seek rest for you, that it might be well with you?" (3:1). Naomi had virtually ignored Ruth when they first entered Bethlehem together. Now she addresses her intimately as "my daughter" and she takes ownership in regard to protecting Ruth's overall well-being: "Should I not seek rest for you, that it might be well with you?"

For Naomi, where once she had a bleak outlook on her future, now there is hope. Where once she seemed only to be thinking about her own misery, now she is thinking about the needs of her daughter-in-law in addition to her own. How did this change in Naomi come about? Naomi and Ruth were introduced to Boaz, one of their redeemers. This is what our Redeemer, Jesus, does for us. When we are introduced to him, by faith, our future opens up. Our *eternal* future opens up. Jesus fills our hearts with future hope. If you are uncertain about your eternal future, come, meet

---

3. Block, *Judges, Ruth*, 680.

Chapter 1: Initiation of the Plan

Jesus. If you come to him by faith, he will give you rest, that it might go well with you. Jesus immediately infuses believers with a sure and certain hope when they come to him in faith. In fact, he pours love into our hearts by his Spirit (Rom 5:5). Jesus does this the moment we come to him. At times, though, he also reintroduces himself into the life of the believer. At times we, like Naomi, allow bitterness, or something else, to create distance between ourselves and our Redeemer. But Jesus is faithful. He is God, the Almighty, who sovereignly draws his people back to himself in accordance with his will, just as Naomi was being led back to her God. And God had done this for Naomi through Boaz.

At this point, Naomi still does not know what the future holds. But one senses a measure of excitement in her voice. She is walking by faith. She is trusting in God but she is also not afraid to take risks at the right time, to say and to do something. As a Christian, trusting in our Redeemer does not mean that we are always passive and inactive. We do not operate in a state of inertia, never taking risks as the occasion requires. Rather, true faith is active faith. This is what Naomi instructs Ruth to do: take a risk. And Ruth is more than willing to do so. Ruth is willing to do so because she, too, is walking by faith: "All that you say I will do" (Ruth 3:5). What is it exactly that Naomi is asking of Ruth?

We should notice here that, for Naomi, in order for things to go well for Ruth, she must marry. Ruth must marry a man, and not just any man—a good man. In this case, that man is Boaz. Thus, Naomi says, "Should I not find rest for you, that it may be well with you? Is not Boaz . . ." (vv. 1–2). Boaz can give her rest. In a marriage to Boaz, it would go well for Ruth. We should also consider how Naomi describes Boaz: "Is not Boaz our relative" (v. 2). Ruth might have responded to this question with "No, actually he is your relative, not mine." But Ruth does not object, and Naomi does not make this distinction. Through her marriage to Naomi's son, and through her continued commitment to Naomi and to Naomi's God, Ruth, though a foreigner, had been incorporated into the life of Israel and into Naomi's family. Yes, the law warned Israelites about associating with gentiles and entering into marriage with gentiles. But why? The Israelites were warned about marriage with people from pagan nations because of the sin and idolatry in the people of these nations. It was the rampant sin among the gentiles that had the potency to influence Israelites in the wrong direction if the marriage bond was shared with them. The sin in pagan peoples was not absolute, however. Ruth was an exception, and there were others. At

Part III: The Threshing Floor

the same time, God's law also made provisions for sojourners, foreigners, that they should be treated as natives. Why? The Israelites were, at one time, sojourners in Egypt. Naomi's family sojourned in Moab (ch. 1). Ruth was introduced to this family during this time. God is free to pluck one of the gentiles out of their realm and give them a sincere and abiding faith in the promises of God, if he so chooses. This is exactly what he had done with Ruth, the woman from Moab. Though she was a foreigner, the Lord brought her near to himself and to his people—to Bethlehem even—the town in which Jesus, the Messiah, would be born. Thus, Boaz's marriage to Ruth was appropriate, and in this particular case, it was even sanctioned and supported by the law of Moses, not prohibited by it. Naomi did not say, "Boaz is my relative." She said, rather, "Boaz is *our* relative."

Next, Naomi gives Ruth several specific commands. Ruth is to first wash herself and anoint herself (with scented oil or perfume), and then she was to put on a cloak and go outside in the night to the threshing floor. The threshing floor was a place where a worker used a large pronged fork to throw piled-up grain up into the air. Typically, the best places for this would be on a rocky and relatively high surface in the open air. The wind would carry away the chaff, the unusable part of the grain harvest, while the heavier grain, the part used in actual food, would fall back down to the hard surface. It is apparent that this place where Boaz would be was a somewhat isolated place away from the city. It is also apparent that Boaz's work at the threshing floor kept him out until the late hours of the night. So much so that he did not return home after he finished. Instead, he stayed there to eat and drink and he also slept through the night there: "Wash therefore and anoint yourself, and put on your cloak and go down to the threshing floor, but do not make yourself known to the man until he has finished eating and drinking. But when he lies down, observe the place where he lies. Then go and uncover his feet and lie down, and he will tell you what to do" (3:3–4).

Naomi, also, has apparently seen Boaz do this and kept a record of his schedule. The first instructions from Naomi to Ruth are not mysterious. There is no secret in what she is attempting to do with her daughter Ruth. Any single woman who is about to meet up with a potential husband will do this. Even a married woman who is getting ready for a date at night with her husband will do these things. Ruth was to bathe herself, put on perfume, grab her coat, and head out the door. The next part, however, could be considered rather strange. Ruth was to wait until Boaz had finished eating and drinking and had fallen asleep. Then, she was to uncover

Chapter 1: Initiation of the Plan

his feet and lay down next to him. The first thing we need to fully appreciate here is that there is nothing in this book that indicates Ruth was doing something inappropriate. The uncovering of the feet at night was a subtle move so that Boaz might wake up and see Ruth there. It would have been rude or dishonorable for Ruth to shake Boaz awake and say to his face, "Will you marry me?" Instead, the gentle persuasion, along with the rest of her actions, were chaste and honorable. Ruth and Naomi are pure in their intentions. Ruth is seeking a husband in Boaz. This is Naomi's goal as well. At the same time, these actions will put Ruth in a vulnerable position. Boaz could potentially take advantage of Ruth or maybe he might not be strong enough to resist the temptation posed by this scenario to go further with Ruth than he ought at this midnight hour. Or Boaz might misinterpret this whole thing and completely reject Ruth. Any of these possible outcomes would leave Ruth spiritually broken and maybe even broken in body as well.

But Ruth and Naomi, walking by faith, trust in the God of Israel. They were trusting in God to sovereignly turn Boaz's heart in the right direction. And they trust Boaz too: "When he lies down, observe the place where he lies. Then go and uncover his feet and lie down, and he will tell you what to do." Ruth fully complies: "All that you say I will do" (v. 5). Ruth trusts in Naomi and she trusts in Boaz, to a certain extent. Had Ruth not come to Bethlehem to take shelter under the wings of the God of Israel? (2:12). She had. Her move to Bethlehem was evidence of this and she continues to give evidence of her faith here.

This dialogue gives us a picture of the kind of relationship Christians have with our Redeemer, Jesus. Jesus, in fact, is revealed in Scripture as the master winnower who will finally "thresh" the entire world one day (Matt 3:12). We see also in the Bible that the Lord uses similar language to describe the marriage covenant into which he entered with Israel. He "washed" her and "anointed" her and became her husband (Ezek 15:8–9). Indeed, Christian marriage vividly displays to each one of us the mystery of the unbreakable marriage bond all believers have with Christ (Eph 5:22–33). What was Ruth doing here? She was preparing herself to meet her husband. And Naomi was hoping to make it as easy as possible for these two to come together in this way.

This is what we do as Christians throughout our entire lives. We are preparing ourselves to meet the bridegroom. We do this by turning away from sin by his grace our whole lives. But we do this in the full freedom we have knowing that we have already been accepted and embraced by him and that we will be fully accepted by him when we *do* meet him again. So, we prepare ourselves, fully trusting in him, that he is good and that he loves us with an eternal love. We have full assurance that he will not harm us nor will he reject us. We know this because he *died* for us. Instead of fleeing to Moab, this family is now trusting in Yahweh. Thus, they have *peace*. Naomi and Ruth do not know what will happen this night. They do not know what the outcome will be. But walking by faith, hiding under the shadow of God's wings, they are both willing to take this risk. Boaz is a redeemer and a noble man. The law of Israel supported this pursuit. So, they move forward with it by faith and in the peace only God can give. We are called to continually do the same.

Like any good romance story, there is a twist that has yet to be revealed. We will see what this is in the coming chapters. But first, we must find out how *Boaz* responds to Ruth's courageous move.

Chapter 2: Execution of the Plan

RUTH 3:6–9

So she went down to the threshing floor and did just as her mother-in-law had commanded her. And when Boaz had eaten and drunk, and his heart was merry, he went to lie down at the end of the heap of grain. Then she came softly and uncovered his feet and lay down.
At midnight the man was startled and turned over, and behold, a woman lay at his feet! He said, "Who are you?" And she answered, "I am Ruth, your servant. Spread your wings over your servant, for you are a redeemer."

AT THE END OF the previous chapter, Naomi and Ruth were discussing how they might initiate the first actions necessary to possibly get Ruth and Boaz married. If Boaz were to marry Ruth, he could redeem this family from childlessness and so prevent the extinction of Elimelech's seed. If Boaz were to marry Ruth, he would also redeem Ruth from widowhood. And though Ruth had already been incorporated into the life and fellowship of Israel, a marriage to Boaz, who was an Israelite by birth, would solidify Ruth's name into the life and history of this chosen nation. Grafted into the vine of Israel, Ruth would become a vital part of Israel's history, and in this case, she would become a vital part in the history of the Messiah.

This is what we see from the Jewish Gospel writer Matthew. Matthew wrote his Gospel primarily with a Jewish audience in mind to show that Jesus is the Christ, the son of David, and the son of Abraham. How does he do this? He does this partly by including a genealogy of Christ at the

Part III: The Threshing Floor

beginning of his Gospel, and in this lineage he includes Ruth: "The book of the genealogy of Jesus Christ, the son of David, the son of Abraham . . . and Salmon the father of Boaz by Rahab, and Boaz the father of Obed by Ruth, and Obed the father Jesse, and Jesse the father of David the king . . . and Jacob the father of Joseph the husband of Mary, of whom Jesus was born, who is called Christ" (Matt 1:1, 5, 16). Ruth's marriage to Boaz and the birth of her son was all part of God's eternal plan that he executed in history. Part of that plan included tremendous suffering for Ruth at the beginning of her life with Naomi's family. This eternal plan, executed by God, was accomplished, though, through Ruth's obedience in Bethlehem as a young widow. This is what we see here.

Before Ruth was able to give birth to her baby Obed, she had to first do this: "So she went down to the threshing floor and did just as her mother-in-law had commanded her" (Ruth 3:6). What was it that Naomi had commanded her to do? She told Ruth to anoint and wash herself, meet Boaz at the threshing floor, and then uncover his feet after he laid down to sleep. After this, she was to lie next to him and wait patiently for further instructions from Boaz. The fifth commandment in Jewish Old Testament law is this: "Honor your father and your mother" (Deut 5:16). This meant that God's people were to properly honor all the relationships between superiors and those whom they served insofar as the parties involved were not led into sin. For example, children were to submit to their parents and show loving obedience to them in the Lord. And in this context, Naomi is essentially Ruth's mother. And the mother is asking her daughter to do something difficult here. Had Ruth chosen instead to be like the Israelite men in the time of the judges, she might have decided to do whatever was right in her own eyes. She might have told Naomi, "No thank you, this move is too risky for me, I will find my own way." Had she done this there might have been no marriage and no Obed.

However, Ruth does not do this. She had committed herself to Naomi before this moment by oath (Ruth 1:16–17). Ruth is not about to back out of her commitment: "All that you say I will do" (3:5). And her actions match her words: "So she went down to the threshing floor and did just as her mother-in-law had commanded her" (v. 6). After Boaz had fallen asleep, we are told "she came softly and uncovered his feet and lay down" (v. 7). This is not an easy task. She is not being asked to pick up groceries at the market. Ruth is being asked to completely open herself up to potential mistreatment and rejection. There were a number of negative possibilities that

Chapter 2: Execution of the Plan

could come as a result of her actions. But she complies and is content with putting her trust in the Lord and placing her future in his hands. She and Naomi were also trusting in the hidden providence of God that Boaz might be led in the right direction.

Now, it is important to understand that Naomi and Ruth were not entering into this plan completely blind. They were certainly taking a risk, but they were not being foolish. Boaz had already shown himself to be a generous and compassionate man. He is hard working and he had been gentle to Ruth and welcomed her. Nevertheless, taking part in a midnight encounter alone with a single man at the threshing floor is risky, regardless of how honorable that man might be. Ruth is willing to take this chance. For Christians, this is the kind of mentality we are called to embrace. We are called to be vulnerable, open before our Lord. Many of us have made serious mistakes in our past. Like Ruth, we have a tremendous amount of suffering that makes up part of our history. While we are not to completely forget the past nor fully ignore whatever consequences may have resulted from our mistakes and sins, we are called by God to continue moving forward with a view toward the resurrection (Phil 3:13–14). We are to continue to do what God calls us to do and to be what God calls us to be. And we are to be content with this. In this way, we properly entrust our futures to God. This is what Ruth did for herself and for her mother-in-law.

We are taken to the actions of Boaz: "And when Boaz had eaten and drunk, and his heart was merry, he went to lie down at the end of the heap of grain" (Ruth 3:7). The writer structures the record of this moment in an ingenious manner. If there was ever an opportunity for Boaz to lapse into a serious moral error, it is found here. Ruth is vulnerable, this much is true. But Boaz is in a vulnerable position too! There is no mysterious meaning here. The writer is clear. Every man knows what this feels like—to reach the end of a long grueling day or week of work that he might be able to enjoy a nice dinner and drink some wine. Boaz then looks with satisfaction upon the fruit of his labor and finds rest. This is what Boaz is doing. His belly is full and his heart is merry with wine (not drunk though). He is finished with the work of the day. The sun has gone down. It is time to relax and treat one's self to some much-needed downtime. In the minds of some men, with only the moon watching, Ruth's overture would be seen as an easy opportunity to take advantage. But this is not who Boaz is. He is a *worthy* man of the tribe of Elimelech and he will prove his worth here: "Then she came softly and uncovered his feet and lay down. At midnight the man was startled and turned over, and behold, a woman lay at his feet!" (v. 8).

This is a shock to him. The writer uses the word *behold* to emphasize this: "Behold, a woman lay at his feet!" Naomi and Ruth's plan had worked. Ruth had approached softly, secretly, and uncovered his feet. She then lay down. This was an attempt to wake him up. The night air apparently touched his toes and startled him so that he did awaken. This move on the part of Ruth was discreet, subtle, honorable, and appropriate. Ruth did not go too far. She did not send the wrong type of message. To be sure, it was a message. But it was a holy message. The gesture of uncovering his feet and lying down next to him is subtle but strong enough to get his attention and communicate Ruth's seriousness about the matter. And it is morally pure.

What happens next is incredible and unexpected. Ruth had been told by Naomi that she should uncover his feet, lie down, and wait for Boaz to tell her what to do. She does all of this and a little bit more. When Boaz wakes up, sees her, and asks about her identity, Ruth takes this midnight opportunity to add her own part to Naomi's original plan. Boaz wakes up and says to the woman laying at his feet, "Who are you?" (v. 9). This is where Ruth gets creative. She says, "I am Ruth, your servant. Spread your wings over your servant, for you are a redeemer." Ruth is imitating her mother-in-law here. In the beginning, Naomi had taken the initiative. Now Ruth does. She takes the initiative with this statement and response.

She announces her identity. At this point in the story, she is no longer *the Moabite woman*, or *the widow from Moab who followed Naomi to Bethlehem*. She is Ruth.[1] And Boaz, in this moment, is to regard her in this way. At the same time, Ruth twice identifies herself as Boaz's servant: "I am Ruth, your servant. Spread your wings over your servant." Ruth, then, humbly submits herself to his leadership and care. As his servant, she will do as Naomi asked her to do and wait for further instructions from Boaz.

Ruth says to him, "Spread your wings over me." Boaz knew what this meant. He had already used similar words in speaking to Ruth: "The LORD repay you for what you have done, and a full reward be given you by the LORD, the God of Israel, under whose wings you have come to take refuge!" (2:12). This phrase from Ruth could also be translated "Spread the corner of your garment over me."[2] In either case, it is midnight; Ruth uncovered Boaz's feet, and they are alone. They met at least once already and so each

---

1. Block, *Judges, Ruth*, 690; Hubbard, *Book of Ruth*, 211.
2. Holladay, *Concise*, 160; Block, *Judges, Ruth*, 691; Hubbard, *Book of Ruth*, 212.

Chapter 2: Execution of the Plan

had knowledge of the other. Ruth also mentions here that Boaz is a redeemer for this family. God uses the same language to describe the marriage covenant he entered into with Israel: "When I passed by you again and saw you, behold, you were at the age for love, and I spread the corner of my garment over you and covered your nakedness; I made my vow to you and entered into a covenant with you, declares the Lord God, and you became mine" (Ezek 16:8). Ruth, then, is employing scriptural language to express her desire that Boaz enter into a marriage covenant with her. She wants him to marry her![3] She wants to be redeemed, through him, by him, for herself, for Naomi, and for God's glory.

"Spread your wings over me" means that she wants Boaz to be fully responsible for her protection and care for the rest of their lives together. She is not there for a moment of passion but for lifelong, faithful, covenant love. For herself and Naomi, redemption is what she is after: "You are a redeemer." What is so masterful about Ruth's response here is that now the focus is on Boaz. Will he spread his wings over her as he should? His character will be tested here. His deepest convictions will come to light. We know what Ruth wants. What will Boaz do?

We are reminded somewhat of the encounter that Mary Magdalene and the other Mary had with Jesus after he was raised from the dead. Jesus said to them: "Do not be afraid" (Matt 28:10). Boaz says the same thing to Ruth here: "Do not fear" (Ruth 3:11). But this is the encounter that all believers have with our Redeemer. Just as Boaz had risen from sleep to find Ruth at his feet, so, too, Jesus has risen from the dead. And we are before him, vulnerable and desiring to be cared for and protected—to be redeemed. The difference, of course, between Boaz and Christ is that Boaz was still sinful. Because of the reality of sin—potential sin in Boaz—Ruth and Naomi could not be entirely certain that he would do the right thing. But Christ is without sin. He has proven himself worthy of our worship and praise. He died for us, in our place, to redeem us. He now stands alive in heaven and we come before him and we say, "Jesus, I am your servant, spread your wings over your servant."

The reader may have missed it but our writer was sure to include a little foreshadowing of possible conflict in this story. Ruth says to Boaz, "Spread your wings over your servant, for you are a redeemer." She did not say, "You are *the* redeemer." Could there be another redeemer? Could there be another who has the right to step in before Boaz and so become Ruth's

---

3. Hubbard, *Book of Ruth*, 212; Ferguson, *Faithful God*, 84; Block, *Judges, Ruth*, 691.

Part III: The Threshing Floor

bride? Could it be that Boaz and Ruth do not end up together after all? We will have to wait and see.

Chapter 3: Response

RUTH 3:10-13

And he said, "May you be blessed by the LORD, my daughter. You have made this last kindness greater than the first in that you have not gone after young men, whether poor or rich. And now, my daughter, do not fear. I will do for you all that you ask, for all my fellow townsmen know that you are a worthy woman. And now it is true that I am a redeemer. Yet there is a redeemer nearer than I. Remain tonight, and in the morning, if he will redeem you, good; let him do it. But if he is not willing to redeem you, then, as the LORD lives, I will redeem you. Lie down until the morning."

THESE VERSES RECORD BOAZ'S initial response to Ruth's actions at midnight at the threshing floor. Boaz had woken up in the middle of the night to find a young woman lying at his feet. At first, he did not know who it was. He asks, "Who are you?" Ruth replies, "I am Ruth, your servant. Spread your wings over your servant, for you are a redeemer" (v. 9). Ruth's words at this point are important. Additionally, what is equally important is Boaz's interpretation of her words. The words of Boaz show that he fully understands what Ruth is asking. The mention of her name in the midst of the midnight darkness tells Boaz that this is the same woman he was curious about earlier. At that time, he asked one of his supervisors about her (2:5-6). He had invited this same young woman to have lunch with him and his other workers (vv. 14-16). She took bread from his hand and she ate until she was satisfied. The writer did not include Ruth's name when

Part III: The Threshing Floor

Boaz had initially asked about her. His supervisor simply replied, "She is the young Moabite woman" (v. 6) and then relayed to Boaz her decision to follow Naomi into Bethlehem from Moab. In the dialogue between Boaz and Ruth in chapter 2, Ruth referred to herself as "a foreigner" and as Boaz's "servant" (vv. 10, 13). But now, here at midnight at the threshing floor, face-to-face with Boaz, she is "Ruth." She is becoming something more to him in this story. And now Boaz, face-to-face with Ruth, is presented with lofty expectations. These expectations come from Ruth and from behind Ruth, for these are the expectations of Naomi as well.

There is tension here. Ruth is alone with a man at midnight, lying down at his feet. We must not forget that this all took place in Israel "in the days when the judges ruled" (1:1). In those days in Israel most men did whatever was right in their own eyes. Most men, at this time, having woken up to a situation like this, probably would have taken advantage of Ruth or they would have rejected her, perhaps even rebuking her harshly for her actions. But Boaz is not like them. He is a *worthy* man (2:1). He is gentle with her. The first words out of his mouth form a prayer: "May you be blessed by the LORD, my daughter" (3:10). He also says, "Do not fear" (v. 11). Regardless of what he says or does after this, these initial words inform Ruth, and the reader of this story, that Boaz is not going to harm her in any way. She is safe before him. Any tension created by the uncertainty of her safety has been relieved.[1]

As we consider the words of Boaz, it is important to appreciate that as soon as Ruth speaks, Boaz knows what she is asking. She mentions that he is a redeemer. He knows what this is. He is familiar with the redemption rights in Israel among families: "And now it is true that I am a redeemer" (v. 12). As Ruth speaks these words, Boaz's mind is flooded with all the knowledge he possesses about Ruth, this situation, and Israelite law. He mentions that he had noticed, and now fully realizes, that Ruth had not pursued a relationship with another man in Judah: "You have not gone after young men, whether poor or rich" (v. 10). In other words, Boaz knows she means to marry him. But he also knows, given her age and situation (she was probably physically attractive), that Ruth could have had her pick of the men in Judah. The reference to the *poor* and the *rich* includes all men

---

1. Block writes, "These opening words are extremely important, for they break the tension in the drama. Now the reader as witness to the drama may relax." *Judges, Ruth*, 692. Also Hubbard, *Book of Ruth*, 213–14.

Chapter 3: Response

and all reasons for marriage.[2] Had Ruth simply wanted to get married to a man for the sake of marriage itself, she could have pursued other men. This statement seems to indicate that she would not have had much trouble finding one.

But it was evident she was aiming for something higher. Boaz pronounces a benediction, a blessing, upon Ruth for her request for marriage. The blessing extends beyond her verbal request and applies also to her prior actions; namely, secretly uncovering his feet and lying down next to him. He commends her faithfulness: "May you be blessed by the Lord, my daughter. You have made this last kindness greater than the first in that you have not gone after young men, whether poor or rich." The blessing extends further still. The *former* kindness he refers to here is likely Ruth's willingness, in the beginning, to follow Naomi to Bethlehem and serve her mother-in-law and her mother-in-law's God. Recall his words to her prior to this moment: "All that you have done for your mother-in-law since the death of your husband has been fully told to me, and how you left your father and mother and your native land and came to a people that you did know before" (2:11). He compares her actions and words at this point with what she had already done.

The *last kindness* to which Boaz refers is the most recent expression of her covenant love, and he says it is greater than what she had done previously. Why? Ruth is forsaking the pursuit of a relationship with one of the other men, so that she might make herself vulnerable and pursue Boaz for the marriage right of redemption. This recent action showed that Ruth was not just thinking about herself in regard to marriage. Certainly, it would not have been altogether unsurprising for Ruth to pursue Boaz in this way. After all, he was a noble and worthy man. He was well respected and honored in the community, and he was a successful businessman. Boaz had shown himself to be generous and kind. But it is also clear that Ruth is thinking of Naomi. Ruth knows a marriage to Boaz would go well for Ruth. But she also had a working knowledge of the right of redemption according to the laws of Israel. She tells Boaz, "You are a redeemer" (3:9). Thus, Ruth was thinking beyond herself to Naomi, to Naomi's former husband's name, to the law of Israel, and to the God of Israel. This is what causes Boaz to respond so favorably to Ruth's words and actions here. This is part of what makes Ruth a *worthy* woman in the eyes of Boaz and in the eyes of the community: "All my fellow townsmen know that you are a worthy woman" (v. 11).

---

2. Hubbard, *Book of Ruth*, 214–15. Block, *Judges, Ruth*, 693.

Part III: The Threshing Floor

The word translated *worthy* is the same word used in chapter 2 to describe Boaz. There he was described as a *worthy* man. Now, Ruth is described as a *worthy* woman. What makes her worthy? The townspeople in Bethlehem, along with Boaz, noticed that she had quietly submitted herself (although a foreigner) to Naomi, to the people of Israel, and to Israel's God. She had done so by humbling herself. She willingly, patiently, and quietly gleaned behind the other Israelite reapers. She worked hard in the fields, as a scavenger essentially, in order to improve her life and the life of her mother-in-law. She did not carelessly and foolishly pursue a relationship with just any man in Judah. She was not loud. She did try to make a name for herself. She humbled herself and became obedient. Now, before Boaz, she continues to do the same. She is taking a risk by placing herself in this position, but she is willing to do so because she is a *worthy* woman. She thinks of the needs of others in addition to her own.

In light of these things, it should not be a surprise that Boaz is enamored by her. He immediately tells her that he is willing to marry her, to redeem her. He even takes an oath: "As the LORD lives, I will redeem you."[3] This oath and the fact that Boaz's promise is set next to the name of Yahweh, the LORD, perhaps gives us a foreshadowing of what will actually happen—Boaz will redeem here. But we are not there yet, we still do not know. If Boaz and Ruth were to be married something else needs to be addressed. And it is something that concerns God's word and its authority.

It is apparent that Old Testament law was being applied in this situation. According to the law of Moses, if an Israelite man who had brothers married an Israelite woman and died with no sons, the law required the brother closest to him in kinship to redeem the widow of the dead man through marriage. This was to be done in order that they might have children together. In effect, the sons from the second marriage would not advance the name of the second brother. The sons born to the second brother would perpetuate the name of the brother who died (Deut 25:5–10). This is most likely the law that is being applied here. To be sure, this is a unique situation, but the divine principles of Deuteronomy are at work.

Boaz says, "There is a redeemer nearer than I" (Ruth 3:12). That is, there is a family member, a relative, other than Boaz, who is closer to Naomi in terms of blood relation. Therefore, according to Israelite law, he, not Boaz, has the first legal right to redeem this family through a marriage to Ruth. For the listener of this story, this information might be devastating.

---

3. Block, *Judges, Ruth*, 696; Hubbard, *Book of Ruth*, 219.

Chapter 3: Response

One would think that after everything we have seen from Boaz and Ruth, this is the moment where Boaz pledges his commitment to her. This is the moment where the first step toward marriage is taken and they are actually married soon after. Instead, Boaz himself introduces *another* man into the story. Another redeemer? What will he be like? Will Ruth actually end up married to someone else? The listener is reeling.

Ruth has bound herself to this situation. She put herself at the mercy of Boaz and has submitted herself completely to the providence of God. We may notice how often Boaz mentions Ruth being redeemed: "If he will redeem you, good; let him do it [redeem]. But if he is not willing to redeem you, then . . . I will redeem you" (v. 13). One way or another Ruth will be redeemed by marriage through one of these men.

It is apparent that Boaz wants to marry Ruth. He cares for her. But here he shows us, and Ruth, that as much as he might have delighted in Ruth at this point, he delighted in the law of the LORD more. Boaz is now the one taking a risk. Boaz is now willing to let whatever dreams he had of marrying Ruth vanish. Why? For the sake of God's word. He wants to marry Ruth but he wants to do so with a clear conscience. That means he must continue to be obedient to God's word and trust in the providence of Yahweh. He is to do this no matter what other desires might be urging him to do something different. For example, he could have bypassed the law and married Ruth never having told the other man of his redemption rights in regard to Ruth and Naomi. This certainly would have been easier.

Boaz did not choose the easy path. And this is part of what makes Boaz a *worthy* man. We are reminded of the words of Jesus: "Whoever does not take his cross and follow me is not worthy of me" (Matt 10:38). The cross that Boaz would bear at this point was unavoidable. He would either redeem Ruth, thus carrying the cross of laying down his life for her in marriage, or he would watch his imagined life with Ruth vanish as another man redeemed her. Either way, Boaz must die to himself and give full allegiance to the authority of God's word.

In the same manner, Ruth has also taken up her cross. She will either bear the cross of serving Boaz in marriage, or she will bear the cross of serving the other redeemer. Either way, Ruth must die to herself and give full allegiance to God's word.

It is astonishing to think that all of this took place at midnight at the threshing floor. Boaz and Ruth are like two shining stars in the midnight sky. And this at a time when the judges ruled (Ruth 1:1). For the Christian, we are given a picture here of the kind of relationship that exists between Christ and his church. We, like Ruth, open ourselves up to the care of our Redeemer. We fully trust in his wisdom. We are to quietly and faithfully humble ourselves before him as his servants. And all the while, we know that our Redeemer loves us and has laid down his life for us. In his time on earth Jesus did not choose the broad path. The word of his Father set his course for the cross. Jesus did not avoid this. He did not turn to the right or to the left. He remained faithful to his Father's word and to his commitment to his bride, the church. As *worthy* as Boaz was, Jesus is more worthy. He is worthy, even, of our worship.

In addition to this, we get a lesson on marriage. Both parties in a Christian marriage are to be committed to God's word. They are to bear their crosses daily and serve one another in love. There is blessing and joy to be found in marriages that operate like this. The rest of the Bible, like that which is seen in Deuteronomy, gives parameters in marriage. If a person is a believer and is married to an unbeliever, the Christian is to do everything in their power to stay married. Unless of course the unbeliever leaves, then the believing spouse is allowed to let them leave (1 Cor 7:12–16). Those who are single and desire to be married should marry in the Lord. They should not be unequally yoked to an unbeliever (1 Cor 7:39; 2 Cor 6:14). Single Christians who desire marriage should wait patiently on the Lord to provide a spouse who is equally yoked as Boaz and Ruth were. Those who are married should keep themselves pure (Heb 13:4). A husband should delight in his wife (Prov 5:18) and a wife should honor her husband (Prov 31:10–12). Both Ruth and Boaz took the word of God seriously. To each of them, marriage and the right of redemption were serious matters, so much so that they were willing to watch their relationship end if that was God's will. This is what Jesus does for us. He promises us redemption and he is faithful to his word.

At this point, both Ruth and Boaz had placed their future together in God's hands. Will God reward them for staying committed to his word?

Chapter 4: Return

RUTH 3:14-18

So she lay at his feet until the morning, but arose before one could recognize another. And he said, "Let it not be known that the woman came to the threshing floor." And he said, "Bring the garment you are wearing and hold it out." So she held it, and he measured out six measures of barley and put it on her. Then she went into the city. And when she came to her mother-in-law, she said, "How did you fare, my daughter?" Then she told her all that the man had done for her, saying, "These six measures of barley he gave to me, for he said to me, 'You must not go back empty-handed to your mother-in-law.'" She replied, "Wait, my daughter, until you learn how the matter turns out, for the man will not rest but will settle the matter today."

THE SECTION BEGINS WITH a record of Ruth's actions subsequent to the conversation she had with Boaz at the threshing floor. Ruth had made herself vulnerable before God and before Boaz. She showed up in the middle of the night at the threshing floor where Boaz was sleeping. Boaz woke up to find Ruth there, and Ruth makes a passionate request of Boaz that he redeem her through marriage. Boaz is honored and would be delighted to marry Ruth. But he delights in God's law. There is a closer redeemer, another Israelite man, and a stranger in this story. If God's law was to be properly honored and obeyed, he must be given the opportunity to redeem Ruth. At this point, Ruth has become even more vulnerable. This is not

Part III: The Threshing Floor

what she might have expected. Of all the possible outcomes that a reader might have thought would materialize, this seems quite unexpected.

Ruth, up to this point, has already done much for Naomi. She took a risk by leaving her homeland, Moab, after the death of her husband (Naomi's son) and the death of her father-in-law Elimelech (Naomi's first husband). She clung to Naomi and followed her to Bethlehem. After entering Bethlehem as a foreigner and a widow, she began to work in the fields of Judah. She had to ask permission of Naomi and the supervisor of the fields if she could do this. She works hard until the end of barley and wheat harvest and she lives with Naomi. Then she does exactly what Naomi asked her to do in the midnight meeting with Boaz at the threshing floor. Naomi told her before she left, "He will tell you what to do" (v. 4).

Naomi, of course, was hoping against hope that Boaz would tell her the steps that needed to be taken in order to marry Ruth and properly redeem her. But this does not happen (initially). Boaz reveals the presence of another redeemer and the legal rights *this man* has according to Israelite law.

Ruth, once again, is faced with a difficult decision. Will she continue in this state of vulnerability? We should pay attention to the last words of Boaz to Ruth in verse 13: "Lie down until the morning." And we should then consider what Ruth actually did: "So she lay at his feet until the morning" (v. 14). Her actions are a mirror reflection of Boaz's words. In other words, she does not back out. She does not stop even though the situation is now changed and is more difficult than she expected. She follows through with her commitment. Ruth will remain obedient to the very end, come what may.

This is what it means to take refuge under the shadow of God's wings. It is opening yourself up to his service completely while trusting in his care in all circumstances. We are told she arose very early the next morning when it was still dark. Boaz is awake, as well, and we see that he is apparently concerned about gossip among the people. He is concerned about Ruth's reputation.[1] Boaz knows full well that Ruth's intentions at the threshing floor were pure and good. But others might think differently if they saw Ruth leaving this place the next morning, knowing Boaz had also been there. Perhaps Ruth was thinking of Boaz's reputation, as well, which is why she woke up so early. Boaz says, "Let it not be known that the woman

---

1. Ferguson, *Faithful God*, 94–95; Block, *Judges, Ruth*, 697. Hubbard writes, "Such a ticklish, potentially embarrassing situation required precautions." *Book of Ruth*, 221.

Chapter 4: Return

came to the threshing floor" (v. 14). There was no need for some imaginary scandal to be dreamed up in Bethlehem and passed around. So, Boaz will say and do whatever he can to protect Ruth's honor.

We are reminded of Joseph's love for Mary, the mother of Jesus.[2] After finding out his wife was pregnant, Joseph, for a moment, thought that she had been unfaithful. They were betrothed but had not yet consummated the marriage in physical intimacy. She was still a virgin but Joseph did not know this. For a moment, all he knew was that his betrothed was with child and that this child could not have been his own. Joseph was a just man. They could not move forward in marriage. But he also did not want to expose his wife to public shame. Though he believed that Mary had been *dis*honorable, he wanted to protect her honor. So, he resolved to divorce her quietly. Such is a man with integrity nourished by obedience to God's word.

Before Ruth and Boaz separate in the early morning darkness, he asks her to do something. He asks her to hold out her cloak or garment.[3] He asks her to do this so that he can give her more food. We should remember here that Boaz had already shown his generosity to her and Naomi before this encounter. He invited Ruth to share a meal with him and his servants at lunchtime (2:14–16). He had his servants set aside bundles of grain for her to glean. Ruth went home that day with a very large load of food for her and Naomi.

Boaz's character does not change. And Ruth's character does not change. He says to her, "Bring the garment you are wearing and hold it out" (3:15). She then does just as Boaz requested. Boaz then fills Ruth's garment with six measures of barley. The text does not inform us about the exact reasons that Boaz did this until Ruth gets back to the city. Ruth returns home and immediately Naomi questions her: "How did you fare, my daughter?" We would do well to notice how the writer describes what happened with Boaz and Ruth: "Then she told her all that the man had done for her" (v. 16). That is what happened. Boaz had served her. Ruth shows up before Boaz and says, "Spread your wings over your servant" (v. 9) and Boaz ends up *serving* Ruth. Boaz and Naomi were concerned about what other men in the field might do to Ruth: "And Naomi said to Ruth, her daughter-in-law, 'It is good, my daughter, that you go out with his young women, lest in another field you be assaulted'" (2:22). Boaz was no such man. He serves Ruth. He takes action to protect Ruth and provide for her.

---

2. See Matt 1:18–25.
3. Block, *Judges, Ruth*, 697; Hubbard, *Book of Ruth*, 221.

Part III: The Threshing Floor

But the writer provides us with a little more here by quoting at least one of Ruth's statements about Boaz: "These six measures of barley he gave to me, for he said to me, 'You must not go back empty-handed to your mother-in-law'" (3:17). Boaz said these words at the threshing floor before they separated. But our writer does not disclose his words until now when Ruth repeats them. Why? It is clear that, generally speaking, Boaz is a generous man. It seems to be just natural for Boaz to give.

But perhaps something else was in Boaz's mind.[4] The six measures of barley and the words he said may have been meant to be received as a not-so-subtle message to Naomi. Boaz is not naïve. He knows what his relationship is with Naomi. He had found out about Ruth and met her. He knew himself to be a redeemer: "It is true I am a redeemer" (v. 12). Before this he had said to Ruth: "All that you have done for your mother-in-law since the death of your husband has been fully told to me" (2:11). The right of redemption was already on his mind, but he also knew there was another man, another redeemer. Perhaps this is the reason why he had not taken any steps to pursue Ruth after they enjoyed lunch together. We are not told. But Ruth had taken the initiative. She shows up at midnight at Boaz's feet requesting that Boaz redeem her. Should we not think that Boaz had at least some inclination that Naomi was behind Ruth's bold first move? It seems rather unlikely that Boaz thought Ruth dreamed up this plan all on her own.

Boaz decides to send a message back to Naomi through Ruth. Carrying the six measures of barley in her shawl, Ruth speaks to Naomi and repeats Boaz's words: "You must not go back empty-handed to your mother-in-law." It is clear the barley was for Ruth and Naomi. If Boaz was being cleverly intentional and if he did think Naomi had some part in what took place at the threshing floor, then we can follow Boaz's actions and words in a clear path. First, Ruth shows up at Boaz's feet requesting redemption. After Boaz wakes up, realizes it is Ruth, and hears her request, he knows Naomi must have been behind this plan. He tells Ruth not to fear. Now, he tells Naomi the same thing. He does this somewhat indirectly through the food gift and his words to Ruth. In a word, Boaz makes it clear to both of them that he will take care of the matter.

This is what Naomi states in the last part: "The man will not rest but will settle the matter today" (3:18). And this is exactly what Boaz did. It is somewhat incredible that Boaz did not rest. He would have needed the

---

4. Block, *Judges, Ruth*, 699–700. See also Hubbard, *Book of Ruth*, 225–26.

rest. He worked hard the previous day. He fell fast asleep and was abruptly wakened by Ruth and a marriage proposal. He then had to think about the matter for the rest of the night. There was not much night left since he and Ruth woke up before the sun came out the next day. Nevertheless, he does not hesitate. God put this matter before him and he immediately responds with hard work and faithfulness.

Even if Boaz did not intend this gift of barley to be a kind of coded message to Naomi, when Naomi heard from Ruth about what Boaz had said and after she sees the gift, she is at peace. She knows Boaz will do what he needs to do to settle the matter quickly that day. So, we are left here with Ruth and Naomi trusting in God's providence and in Boaz's leadership.

From here forward, Naomi and Ruth have less prominence in the story. Ruth is no longer central in the story, and Naomi does not speak in chapter 4. For Christians, what we have in these final images of Ruth and Naomi is a picture of what our posture should be like before our Redeemer, Jesus Christ. Ruth and Naomi had fully committed themselves to the care of Boaz. They would patiently wait while he worked hard to settle the matter of their redemption. The difference between us and these two women is that Ruth and Naomi did not know how it all would turn out. As we are led by Christ, the matter of our redemption has been settled. Our Redeemer died for us. By his death, he saved us. As we look to the cross, the message we should receive from his death is that the matter is settled—you have been redeemed. Christ does not rest. He is always working for our good. He intercedes for us by his Spirit and he rules over heaven and earth.

Ruth and Naomi were at peace. But we should not think that they could completely stop what they had been doing up until this point. Ruth and Naomi would still have responsibilities and activities in which to engage. But in regard to Ruth and Naomi's immediate fate, the story makes it abundantly clear that Boaz must settle the matter of redemption. The full responsibility of redemption belongs to him. This is what Jesus is to his people—our Redeemer. No one else can save.

For those of us who enjoy good books and stories, we should recognize the mastery of the Holy Spirit in telling this particular piece of redemptive history. It is somewhat agonizing to have to wait with Ruth and Naomi to see what happens. But this is what a good writer does. He prepares the reader for a climactic ending.

Part IV: Redemption and Royalty

Chapter 1: A Name Removed

RUTH 4:1-6

Now Boaz had gone up to the gate and sat down there. And behold, the redeemer, of whom Boaz had spoken, came by. So Boaz said, "Turn aside, friend; sit down here." And he turned aside and sat down. And he took ten men of the elders of the city and said, "Sit down here." So they sat down. Then he said to the redeemer, "Naomi, who has come back from the country of Moab, is selling the parcel of land that belonged to our relative Elimelech. So I thought I would tell you of it and say, 'Buy it in the presence of those sitting here and in the presence of the elders of my people.' If you will redeem it, redeem it. But if you will not, tell me, that I may know, for there is no one besides you to redeem it, and I come after you." And he said, "I will redeem it." Then Boaz said, "The day you buy the field from the hand of Naomi, you also acquire Ruth the Moabite, the widow of the dead, in order to perpetuate the name of the dead in his inheritance." Then the redeemer said, "I cannot redeem it for myself, lest I impair my own inheritance. Take my right of redemption yourself, for I cannot redeem it."

IN THE PREVIOUS CHAPTER, most of the activity recorded took place at midnight at the threshing floor. Then the scene shifted to Bethlehem and to what Ruth and Naomi discussed the next day when Ruth returned home. In their discussion the focus of the story shifts entirely to Boaz. Naomi said to

Part IV: Redemption and Royalty

Ruth, "Wait, my daughter, until you learn how the matter turns out, for the man will not rest but will settle the matter today" (3:18). At this point the reader is left wondering how Boaz will settle the matter. Perhaps Ruth and Naomi were wondering the same thing. Regardless of what these widows were thinking, here at the beginning of chapter 4, Ruth and Naomi disappear from the story's action. To be sure, there are words spoken about them, but the writer makes it clear that it is now time for Boaz, and Boaz alone, to do his job. He will settle the matter of redemption. As a gō'ēl he must accomplish all that is necessary to do just this—redeem.

We should pause here to think about the role of Boaz and how every Christian man may learn from him. Boaz wakes up in the middle of the night and in God's providence has a tremendous responsibility laid out before him. He does not hesitate, even on shortened sleep. He wakes up before dawn, gives Ruth more food gifts, and returns to the city. In particular, he returns to the gates of the city so that he might settle this urgent matter. In a word, Boaz gets to work. He is active. He produces. We may recall here what Naomi said about him: "The man will not rest." The opposite of rest is work. As a *worthy* man, this is Boaz's primary calling, to work. There is joy to be found here. This was the original mandate given to Adam in the garden before sin entered the world: "The LORD God took the man and put him in the garden of Eden to work it and keep it" (Gen 2:15). Eve was to be his helper in this. Thus, women in the church are to be active as well. The woman of Proverbs 31 seems to be everywhere all at once. The text buzzes with activity from this sister in the LORD: "She looks well to the ways of her household and does not eat the bread of idleness" (Prov 31:27). For men in the church, though, we are to lead the way in not *eating the bread of idleness*. Boaz does just this. He gets to work. And he does this not knowing what the outcome will be. But he knows he must do this. He must work at the gate for his potential bride-to-be, Ruth, and for Naomi. So, the very next day, Boaz goes to the city's gate.

We see immediately that Boaz is not alone. The LORD is with him. In fact, the LORD was ahead of him preparing the way. Boaz sits down at the gate and we see the word *behold* again in this story: "And behold, the redeemer, of whom Boaz had spoken, came by" (Ruth 4:1). This is not by chance. The god of chance does not exist. From all eternity, the God of Israel ordained that the other redeemer would walk by Boaz at this precise moment. This is why Boaz was there. He needed to address this particular

Chapter 1: A Name Removed

man, along with the elders of the city, if he were to take Ruth as his bride. And he would need to do this in an official capacity.

Official judgments were made at the city's gate.[1] This is not unlike the official meetings that take place among the leaders of a local church. Leaders in a local setting sit down to make official judgments in regard to the members of the church, the church's worship, and other church-related matters. We might also think of meetings of a city council or a state senate. Courtroom meetings may be included in this, as well. The decisions that are made at these meetings are formal. They are legally binding decisions made before witnesses who confirm what decisions were made. This is the kind of sit-down meeting in which Boaz participated. He sat down at the gate of Bethlehem and called a formal meeting in order that he might deal with this particular matter.

Immediately, God provided Boaz with the redeemer he was after. He then calls ten elders of the city and has them sit down. One can easily see here the respect that Boaz must have garnered over time with the men of the city. They are not hesitant to oblige Boaz's request. Boaz, then, addresses the other man, the other redeemer, and gets straight to the point. In this initial speech he sums up the situation:[2]

> Naomi, who has come back from the country of Moab, is selling the parcel of land that belonged to our relative Elimelech. So I thought I would tell you of it and say, "Buy it in the presence of those sitting here and in the presence of the elders of my people." If you will redeem it, redeem it. But if you will not, tell me, that I may know, for there is no one besides you to redeem it, and I come after you. (vv. 3–4)

We would do well to notice here that Boaz does not mention Ruth in the first part of his speech. This is significant. For now, the other redeemer only knows about the land.[3] So, with only the land in mind, the other redeemer says, "I will redeem it" (v. 4). Again, he does not yet know about the obligation to Ruth. Then Boaz mentions what would become a deal-breaker: "The day you buy the field from the hand of Naomi, you also

---

1. Block writes, "The citizens would recognize this as an official act; he had arrived for legal business." *Judges, Ruth*, 705. See also Hubbard, *Book of Ruth*, 232–33.

2. Block writes, "It seems Boaz wasted no time in getting to the heart of the matter." *Judges, Ruth*, 708.

3. Hubbard, *Book of Ruth*, 238; Ferguson, *Faithful God*, 113.

acquire Ruth the Moabite, the widow of the dead, in order to perpetuate the name of the dead in his inheritance" (v. 5).

Let us consider the difference in character between Boaz and this man. They are both men, but Boaz responded to Ruth's request for redemption with generous and immediate action. This man responds with immediate self-protection. He flees from this responsibility as quickly as he can: "I cannot redeem it" (v. 6). Two times he says this phrase: "I cannot redeem it." And what is the reason this man gives for not being able to redeem? He says, "I cannot redeem it for myself, lest I impair my own inheritance." The word *myself* identifies his focus. He is concerned about his own name, his own property, and his own reputation. This is what he cared about.

We may notice what Boaz called Ruth. She is Ruth the Moabite. By blood she was a gentile. She was of Moabite stock, but adopted into the family of Israel. But for this man, apparently, marriage to Ruth the Moabite might hurt his reputation. It might threaten his future and his inheritance. We are not told the details of what this man was thinking at this time. That he backs out of the deal, however, after Boaz mentions the requirements regarding Ruth tells the reader much about his character. The Bible speaks, too, about his focus. This man was concerned about his name and his own inheritance. But in the end, what happens to his name? His name is not mentioned. God's word is silent here. He is forgotten.

Alternately, Boaz's focus is away from himself and on others. In fact, he was there at the gate for Ruth and for Naomi to settle the matter of redemption. He was concerned for their welfare and for the name of the dead, Elimelech. In verse 3, Boaz refers to Elimelech as *our* relative. In verse 5, he mentions marriage to Ruth and then refers to Elimelech two more times. He calls Ruth the widow of the dead. That is, the widow of Elimelech. Additionally, he refers to Elimelech's inheritance and his name in this way: "In order to perpetuate the name of the dead in his inheritance."

In order to fully appreciate what is being said here we need to consider the law of God. There is not a written law in the Old Testament that pertains specifically to a situation like this.[4] But it seems as though the spirit of Deut 25 was applied.[5] Verse 5 of that chapter reads, "If brothers dwell together, and one of them dies and has no son, the wife of the dead man shall not be married outside the family to a stranger. Her husband's brother shall go in to her and take her as his wife and perform the duty of a husband's brother

---

4. Hubbard, *Book of Ruth*, 188–89; Block, *Judges, Ruth*, 674–75.
5. Hubbard, *Book of Ruth*, 188–89; Block, *Judges, Ruth*, 674–75.

Chapter 1: A Name Removed

to her." In this law, if an Israelite man had a wife and he died without sons, the widow of the dead man was to marry the next of kin—namely, the brother. In cases like this, it would be the brother's responsibility to marry his dead brother's widow so that they might have sons together. The sons would perpetuate the name of the deceased brother.

Thus, the sons of the new marriage would be for the dead brother. They would perpetuate his name instead of that name becoming, in a sense, dead and forgotten by death. His name and inheritance would be resurrected, as it were, through the marriage of the brother and the widow. It is clear here that Elimelech did not have brothers (at least no brothers that were alive). But he had male relatives close enough in blood relation who were responsible for acquiring Ruth and the land. The two relatives were Boaz and this man.

These things were important to an Israelite in the ancient Near East—one's seed, name, and land. The covenant promises rested upon the continuance of the name of Abraham through his children. These promises given to the children of Abraham included a land inheritance, a portion of the promised land. To lose one's name in Israel meant the family could also lose land. This is what was at stake here—Elimelech's name and inheritance. Would his name and inheritance die with the deaths of Naomi and Ruth as widows? Or would one of these men in the story lay down their life for the sake of another? The answers are given here. The nameless redeemer says, "I cannot redeem it." Boaz told Ruth the night before this, "As the LORD lives, I will redeem you." This is what he had come to the gate of the city to do. He came here to fulfill his commitments and remain faithful to his vow.

We are reminded of another story in the Bible that tells of two men in history. The first man was Adam. He had a bride he was to care for and protect. He had land to work. He was also to protect this land from invasion. When the serpent showed up Adam shirked his responsibilities. He refused to step in front of Eve, confront the devil, and trample him underfoot. He essentially said, "I cannot protect you; I cannot listen to God's word." He did this because he would have had to enter into spiritual combat with the devil. He chose the easy way—self-protection—the way of death. The other man—the second man, Jesus Christ, our Redeemer and the greater Boaz—says, "I will redeem her." Jesus as our Redeemer then enters into this dark world, shattered by sin and under the dominion of death and the devil. He enters a world with widows and orphans. He takes on human flesh like ours, yet without sin, and he engages in spiritual combat with Satan. In this conflict he dies, laying down his life to redeem us, to revive us, raise us up from the dead that he might secure for his people a future and an inheritance. Jesus, by laying down his life for the sake of others, bought back what the first man had lost because of the first man's desire for self-protection.

To be sure, Boaz is blessed as well as he denies himself for Ruth, Naomi, and Elimelech. The LORD rewards him for his faithfulness and self-sacrifice. But only after he addressed the matter head-on. This is what God's people, both men and women, are to do. We follow the greater Boaz, Jesus Christ, in that we suffer unto glory. We deny ourselves *now* as we look forward to a heavenly reward *later*.

Boaz has won the victory. He confronted the man who might have foiled this romance and he came out the winner, the redeemer. Boaz will marry Ruth! And all of it is open and honest, blessed by God and approved by his word. As Boaz and Ruth make themselves vulnerable before God and submit to his word, they will move forward in love with a clear conscience and with joy, all to the glory of God. The reader may finally exhale. Boaz and Ruth's romance will be consummated in marriage.

Chapter 2: A Name Redeemed

RUTH 4:7-10

Now this was the custom in former times in Israel concerning redeeming and exchanging: to confirm a transaction, the one drew off his sandal and gave it to the other, and this was the manner of attesting in Israel. So when the redeemer said to Boaz, "Buy it for yourself," he drew off his sandal. Then Boaz said to the elders and all the people, "You are witnesses this day that I have bought from the hand of Naomi all that belonged to Elimelech and all that belonged to Chilion and to Mahlon. Also Ruth the Moabite, the widow of Mahlon, I have bought to be my wife, to perpetuate the name of the dead in his inheritance, that the name of the dead may not be cut off from among his brothers and from the gate of his native place. You are witnesses this day."

THIS SECTION IS HEADING toward Boaz's speech to the witnesses of the court proceedings. That speech begins in verse 9: "Then Boaz said to the elders and all the people . . ." Before we get there, the writer gives us a side note explaining legal transactions in ancient Israel. It seems apparent that this custom may have been unfamiliar to the original readers of this book. The writer mentions "former times in Israel." This custom is certainly unfamiliar to us today, so this side note is helpful. There are two things that this explanation does. First, by detailing the legal procedure and what took place in court this day the writer confirms for us what was in the other redeemer's heart. His removal from the story and from the history of Judah,

Part IV: Redemption and Royalty

King David, and the Messiah was legitimate. The first redeemer was not coerced nor forced into this decision. His mind was on his own land, his own reputation. When Ruth the Moabite was mentioned in the deal, he no longer wanted anything to do with the redemption of Naomi's land. He feared union with a gentile might impair his own inheritance (v. 6). So, he said to Boaz, "I cannot redeem it." He further confirmed this by saying, "Take my right of redemption yourself." His actions in court before witnesses confirm his words. By his actions and his words his name is forgotten. He was part of the story for a moment, but he quickly removed himself.

Secondly, this explanatory section in verse 7 connects what took place here in court with an ancient law in Deuteronomy. First, we would do well to appreciate the significance of the nonverbal gesture mentioned here. Removing the sandal and giving it to Boaz signifies just what it says: "to confirm a transaction." Boaz possessing the man's sandal, along with the other man's testimony before the witnesses, was like having a signed document in his hand.[1] The removal of the sandal was a formal act with legal authority. As we saw in the previous chapter, Deut 25 deals with a man who is the closest brother to a dead man. This man's brother died with no sons to carry forward his name. It is now expected, according to the law of God, that this man will marry his brother's wife in order to build up, through children, the house of the dead brother. If this man refused to marry his brother's widow, then the widow was to make this known to the elders of the city. The elders were then to call this man to a council. If he said, "I do not wish to take her," then the brother's wife, in that formal meeting, would pull his sandal off his foot and spit in his face (Deut 25:5–10). All of this would take place at the gate of the city.

It seems that this, in a way, is the kind of case being arbitrated in Bethlehem with Boaz and this other man. The details are different, to be sure. But this is important if we are to understand how Israelite elders dealt with a man who refused to fulfill his obligations as a redeemer of his brother's line. It was a shameful thing to neglect obligations and responsibilities in Israel in a case like this, hence the spitting in the face. The other consequence is that the man who refused was forgotten. The first redeemer in the story who chose not to go through with this is not mentioned by name. He is forgotten while Boaz's name is remembered for generations. It was also

---

1. Ferguson writes, "It appears to have been the rough equivalent of signing the legal deed and shaking hands on the contract. Thus the transaction becomes binding." *Faithful God*, 114. See also Block, *Judges, Ruth*, 717–18.

Chapter 2: A Name Redeemed

customary in a transaction like this for the man, in this case Boaz, to give a speech in the presence of all those who were there.[2] That speech would serve as an interpretation of what had just taken place. This is what we see in Boaz's speech, and it is the last time we hear from him in this book.[3] The speech begins with Boaz addressing all the people at the gate, including the elders: "Then Boaz said to the elders and all the people, 'You are witnesses this day.'" He says this phrase again at the end of his speech in verse 10: "You are witnesses this day." This meant that at any moment from this point on the witnesses could give testimony on the case's legal merit. Their witness then had a measure of authority. What did they witness? Boaz, under the inspiration of the Holy Spirit, begins with the land: "You are witnesses this day that I have bought from the hand of Naomi all that belonged to Elimelech and all that belonged to Chilion and to Mahlon."

With the reference to the land, we are reminded of the deaths of these three men. This was part of Naomi's history and part of Ruth's history. Now it is part of Boaz's history. The possession of the land and the rights of the land inheritance passed from Elimelech to Chilion and Mahlon at his death. But Chilion and Mahlon both died. Thus, the possession of the land passed to Naomi because she had no more sons. The land was hers to hand over: "From the hand of Naomi" (Ruth 4:9). Now that land belongs to Boaz because he redeemed it: "I have bought." Although Boaz cared about the land, this was not his primary concern. He did not need the land. He had land and servants (ch. 2). He was not concerned about his reputation. Even though Ruth was a Moabite, a gentile, Boaz made sure that she was protected. Thus, reputation and land were not his concern. What did he care about? Ruth! "Also Ruth the Moabite, the widow of Mahlon I have bought to be my wife." His eye was on Ruth. He loved the LORD and he loved her. And he showed his love for her, not by this speech primarily, but by his actions. This is why Boaz was at the gate of the city this day, to settle the matter of redemption in regard to his wife, Ruth. He leaves mention of Ruth for the end of his speech, emphasizing this point.[4] As they raised children together, Boaz and Ruth would "perpetuate the name of the dead in his inheritance, that the name of the dead may not be cut off from among his brothers and from the gate of his native place" (4:10).

---

2. Block, *Judges, Ruth*, 719.
3. Block, *Judges, Ruth*, 719.
4. Block writes, "It is obvious from the construction of the sentence, however, that Ruth was his primary goal." *Judges, Ruth*, 720.

In a word, Boaz was laying down his life for Ruth and he was laying down his life for his relative, Elimelech. We may consider how many times Elimelech is mentioned by name or indirectly referred to in this speech: "I have bought from the hand of Naomi all that belonged to Elimelech . . . to perpetuate the name of the dead in his inheritance, that the name of the dead may not be cut off from among his brothers and from the gate of his native place." Boaz was willing to lose his own name and his own reputation for the sake of his brother/kinsman Elimelech, to revive his brother's name and raise it from the dead. And this by way of children with his bride-to-be, Ruth. He did this for the sake of Israel and for God's glory.

This is how the witnesses receive this speech from Boaz. Their response to what Boaz said was focused entirely on this—*Ruth*, and the children she would bear. "May the LORD make the woman, who is coming into your house, like Rachel and Leah, who together built up the house of Israel . . . because of the offspring that the LORD will give you by this young woman" (vv. 11–12). The woman, Ruth, his bride, his beloved, a family, children—*this* is what Boaz, the true redeemer, was after. He shows that he was more than willing to assume the sacrifice required of him to care for Ruth and fulfill his obligations as the redeemer.

What we have here, in shadow form, is where Jesus's heart was when he came to this earth. As God, Jesus owns all of heaven and earth. He created it. He didn't need land or money. He did not come to be served but to serve. His heart was on his people, purchasing us, acquiring us to be his bride, all to the glory of his Father. He has done this by laying down his life for us. By dying in our place on the cross he purchased us. This is what the Bible gives as an infallible interpretation of Christ's death, which took place *outside* the gates of the city. Let us look to the cross and to the judgment rendered there. As we do, let us remember that Christ now stands raised from the dead and says to all of heaven and earth, "I have purchased her to be my bride."

Chapter 3: A Name Renowned

RUTH 4:11-12

Then all the people who were at the gate and the elders said, "We are witnesses. May the Lord make the woman, who is coming into your house, like Rachel and Leah, who together built up the house of Israel. May you act worthily in Ephrathah and be renowned in Bethlehem, and may your house be like the house of Perez, whom Tamar bore to Judah, because of the offspring that the Lord will give you by this young woman."

THIS SECTION RECORDS THE response of the elders and the witnesses to the court proceedings and to Boaz's speech. Often, a high-profile court case will attract a crowd. This is what had happened in the proceedings that took place at the gate of the city of Bethlehem. Boaz had summoned ten elders of the city and the other redeemer. Their presence was certainly required in order to make the meeting legal. But the activities at the gate involving Boaz, Naomi, and Ruth had attracted a gathering of citizens of Bethlehem. They may not have known this at first, but their curiosity and attendance at the meeting caused them, in the end, to be officially involved in the final decision, its interpretation and its confirmation. That was the last thing Boaz said to the elders and all the people who were at the gate: "You are witnesses this day" (v. 10). What this meant for Boaz was that there were witnesses who could confirm that he had taken Ruth to be his wife. This included all the obligations and responsibilities that come along with this. Boaz, as a worthy man, was willing to publicly take on these responsibilities and to be held accountable to the witnesses there. This all takes place while the other redeemer vanishes into the background.

The witnesses collectively respond: "We are witnesses." That is, they respond favorably to Boaz's assertion. They, too, confirm that what they witnessed has lasting legal ramifications and they are also willing to take on the responsibilities as witnesses.[1] We have seen that Boaz and Ruth are exceptional people, honorable, worthy, and righteous, by all human accounts. Nevertheless, the witnesses' collective speech teaches us something. It teaches us what the psalmist teaches us: "Unless the LORD builds the house, those who build it labor in vain" (Ps 127:1).[2] Boaz and Ruth are still human servants, called by God to be involved in his program of redemption in history. If this marriage is to produce the intended outcome—namely, a son to perpetuate the name of the dead—then God the LORD must do it. So, the witnesses pronounce a prayer of blessing upon Boaz. And in the power of the Spirit, they end up prophesying as well. This is what was taking place here in Bethlehem over three thousand years ago. The witnesses pray for Boaz and they prophesy about the future of Boaz and Ruth: "May the LORD make the woman, who is coming into your house, like Rachel and Leah" (Ruth 4:11).

The witnesses focus their prayer on Ruth's possible children with Boaz. They say essentially, "May your families be like the families of Rachel and Leah." This is what they meant when they say that Rachel and Leah "built up the house of Israel." Rachel and Leah were Jacob's wives. The sons that were born to these two women comprised the twelve tribes of Israel, the twelve *houses* of Israel: Reuben, Simeon, Levi, Judah, and all the rest. To put it another way, the twelve sons of Rachel and Leah made up the foundation of the people of God. The witnesses were praying then that God would grant Ruth, a gentile by birth, a place right alongside Rachel and Leah as a mother of the Israelite nation. Rachel and Leah were regarded as virtual queens in Israel. The same now holds true for Ruth. The witnesses bring into view the honor and respect these women had in the eyes of the people of God. They were faithful mothers to sons, mothers of children. This is what Ruth was destined to be—a mother to Boaz's son.

The next thing they pray for is that the LORD would make Boaz's house worthy of honor and that the LORD would make his name famous in Israel. The first redeemer was worried about his own reputation, so he would not

---

1. Block, *Judges, Ruth*, 721; Hubbard, *Book of Ruth*, 258.
2. Block, *Judges, Ruth*, 721.

Chapter 3: A Name Renowned

marry Ruth. As a result, that which he feared happened—his name is forgotten. Boaz was not concerned about his reputation. He was concerned about the name of his ancestor Elimelech. And yet it is Boaz, *his name*, that becomes famous forever among the people of God. Because of his humility, the name of Boaz is worthy of honor. We are reminded of Jesus's words: "Whoever humbles himself will be exalted" (Matt 23:12). He will be exalted by God. This is what the Lord did with Boaz. Boaz humbled himself and God exalted him.

The witnesses also pray that the Lord would make Boaz's house like the house of Perez, the son of Tamar and Judah. The situation between Judah and Tamar was unique, to be sure, but there are similarities with what we have between Boaz and Ruth. Both stories involved widows with no sons. Both stories involved men who refused to honor the law of God and fulfill the requirements of an Israelite family member toward a childless widow in the family bloodline (Gen 38:1–30). Both stories included two women, Tamar and Ruth, who proved to be more righteous than some of the Israelite men involved.

Tamar was married to one of Judah's wicked sons. He died without an heir. The next son refused to take Tamar as his wife and produce children with her. So, the Lord put him to death. Judah promised Tamar the third son in marriage, but as the third son grew up Judah was not faithful to his promise. Tamar saw this happening, so she disguised herself and tricked Judah into having a child with her. She gave birth to a son, Perez. He is mentioned here. And what became of Perez's children? From Perez's line came strong, honorable men, leaders in Israel: Caleb, Nahshon (a prince), Boaz, and the most renowned name of all at the time this book was written, King David. Thus, the genealogy at the end of the book begins with Perez and ends with David (Ruth 4:18–22).

Though the prayer and blessing here centers on Boaz and Ruth, it is ultimately a prayer that God would give Ruth a son. Really, it is a Spirit empowered prophecy.[3] The witnesses say, "May your house be like the house of Perez, whom Tamar bore to Judah, because of the offspring that the Lord will give you by this young woman." This is something the Lord would do, and in the power of the Spirit the witnesses testify to this.

There is another lesson here for us about how important a godly family is in the eyes of God. In the wisdom of God, the history of Israel's

---

3. Block writes, "They had come to witness but they left prophesying." *Judges, Ruth*, 724.

redemption included and really centered upon the faithfulness of families like this one. We know that this is all about a son being born to Boaz and Ruth when we read, "Because of the offspring that the LORD will give you by this woman." That son would have a family of his own, and so on until David, Ruth's great grandson, was born. They may not have been able to fully understand this here, but Boaz and Ruth's faithfulness would play an integral part in the making of Israel's great king. God's wisdom does not stop here however. For it was not just Israel's history that revolved around the history of a family, but all world history. The history of the entire world centers upon a son being born to a woman. The woman was Mary, Joseph's betrothed. The son was the Lord Jesus Christ, redeemer of the world. Indeed, Christ's genealogy traces back to David and on to Boaz and Ruth (Matt 1:1–17; Ruth 4:18–22). Boaz and Ruth could not have seen how important their son would be in the history of redemption. Such is God's infinite and unsearchable wisdom.

This text also affirms that *God* gives men and women children. Every birth is a gift from him. He forms each child personally in the womb of the mother: "Because of the offspring that the LORD will give you by this woman" (v. 12). Ruth's great grandson, David, would reaffirm this truth later on in one of his many songs: "For you formed my inward parts; you knitted me together in my mother's womb" (Ps 139:13). Ultimately, the gift of childbirth that is referenced in this prayer points to a miracle. It foreshadows the great manifestation of God's power to give life in the womb in impossible circumstances. That miracle is the virgin birth. The conception of Jesus by the Holy Spirit in the womb of Mary, apart from any involvement by Joseph, is the miracle to which all these births pointed. God gave Obed to Ruth. Then David was born. Then, miraculously, he gave the world his Son through the virgin Mary.

For the people of God today, we would do well to remember that the LORD is still raising up children of Boaz—spiritual children. He does this through faithful Christian families. We should continually pray that Christ's name would be made famous through us and through our children and our children's children, as we raise them in our homes. And that is where we are headed next in the story, to the home of Boaz and Ruth.

Chapter 4: Arrival of a Son

RUTH 4:13

So Boaz took Ruth, and she became his wife. And he went in to her, and the Lord gave her conception, and she bore a son.

WE HAVE APPROACHED THE climax of the story. Everything we have witnessed and heard about from the very beginning was leading up to this moment: "So Boaz took Ruth, and she became his wife." From the very first word in chapter 1, the writer had this moment in view. It is the climax, the high point in the story. Now that Boaz and Ruth are married, we can look back to the beginning, and consider again the first parts of the story in light of the ending.

The events of Ruth took place in "the days when the judges ruled" (1:1). One word can describe these days—darkness. It was a time of spiritual darkness in the people of God. In the days when the judges ruled in Israel, sin and depravity, for the most part, prevailed. If you were an Israelite in these days, you would look around at God's people and see this: "Everyone did what was right in their own eyes" (Judg 21:25). We also see that it was a time of emptiness: "In the days when the judges ruled there was a famine in the land." The land, Judah, had been emptied of food. This famine pushed Elimelech and his family (Naomi and her two sons) out of Judah and into the nation of Moab. In the face of starvation and emptiness, Elimelech sought refuge in a gentile nation. Instead of being filled, though, there was more emptiness.

Part IV: Redemption and Royalty

Elimelech died, thus Naomi was emptied of a husband. After taking to themselves Moabite wives, both of Naomi's sons died. Naomi was now emptied of her sons. The writer summed this emptiness up in one verse in chapter 1: "The woman was left without her two sons and her husband" (Ruth 1:5). In this way, Naomi's experience encapsulated the experience of all of Israel at this time. Naomi had been bereft of a future. For Judah and Israel, the land was partly barren. Good, strong leadership was barren. The people of God in general were bereft of righteousness. These were the people who were supposed to bring blessing to the nations. Now, there was just darkness and emptiness.

And yet, the light had not been completely extinguished. In Boaz and Ruth, and in how the LORD was preparing the way for these two shining lights to come together, we learn a valuable lesson from this book. This lesson was for the people of God in the generation when the book was written, and it is a lesson for every generation of God's people, including ours today.

The lesson is this: God brings light out of darkness and he brings life out of death.[1] We are reminded of the words of John. At the beginning of his Gospel, speaking of Jesus the Messiah, the Son of David, who came into the world, John says this: "In him was life, and the life was the light of men. The light shines in the darkness, and the darkness has not overcome it" (John 1:4–5). No matter how much darkness there is in the world, no matter how much emptiness, God is always at work, bringing life into a situation surrounded by much death. God is always at work to fill those who are empty. He is Father to the fatherless and a protector of widows. Even in Naomi's widowhood, God was preparing for her a worthy man who would become her son-in-law and redeemer. *Boaz* would fill the void left by the deaths of Mahlon and Chilion, and God would do even more. He would fill Naomi all the more with a grandson, Obed. She would be a nurse to him.

In Ruth's widowhood, God was preparing the same man, Boaz, to fill the void left by the death of Ruth's husband, Mahlon. God sovereignly plucked Ruth out of a pagan people and gave her a heart to leave her people and her land and go to a foreign place. As a reward for her faithfulness, God filled her with a new people and a new land. He filled her with his word and his promises. He gave her, through Boaz, the grandfather of Israel's coming king. Thus, Ruth was given a place among the noble women in redemptive history. Sin was not victorious in Israel; darkness did not prevail. *God* prevailed as he always does. In a story filled with so much suffering and death,

---

1. Ferguson, *Faithful God*, 39.

Chapter 4: Arrival of a Son

Boaz and Ruth and their son to be born were living proof that God is Lord and he is good. The light was coming into the world and the darkness has not overcome it.

There are times in our lives as Christians that we feel emptied by God. This may be due to death, another's sin, our own sin, or just the ever-present sin and darkness in this world. At times this can burden us. These words, "Boaz took Ruth and she became his wife" should give us hope. They should inspire us to persevere and to wait patiently on the Lord. He is good and his steadfast love endures forever.

The Lord, Yahweh, is mentioned many times in this book, but there are only two times where the narrator has the Lord as the subject of the action.[2] The first time is found in chapter 1. There we are told Naomi sets out from Moab to return to Judah with her daughters-in-law, all three of them widows. They decide to return because "The Lord had visited his people and given them food" (v. 6). That is, the Lord caused the land to be fruitful again where once it was barren. The Lord opened it up again and filled the land with fruit and grain. The second time the narrator uses the Lord as subject of the action is found here: "So Boaz took Ruth, and she became his wife. And he went in to her, and the Lord gave her conception, and she bore a son" (4:13). "Boaz went in to her" is a reference to the consummation of marriage through physical intimacy. This would take place when the husband went into the bedroom chamber of his wife. In God's infinite wisdom, this is the natural way that children come into this world. A man and woman are united physically (a union intended to take place within the covenant of marriage). The woman conceives and gives birth. God established it this way and there is no way around it unless God intervenes. Ever since Adam and Eve were created, this intervention has happened only one time.

We will consider that unique birth in a moment but for now our focus will be on the Lord's action in this verse: "The Lord gave her conception." The Lord filled her belly with the first spark of life. A child began to grow and to be formed in her womb. Now, Ruth had been married before, to Mahlon, but they did not have children because God did not give them children. Every conception reveals the wisdom and power of God. We are told in Ps 139 that God personally forms each child in the womb of his mother. Every child that has ever come into the world, even one that does not see the light of day, is wonderfully made by God. The power to produce

---

2. Block, *Judges, Ruth*, 725.

PART IV: REDEMPTION AND ROYALTY

children is ultimately not in the hands of men and women. We know this from this passage and from other passages where we are told God *closed* the womb of a woman. We are told this in regard to Hannah: "The LORD had closed her womb" (1 Sam 1:5). For Christians today, this is how we are to regard all children, especially children in the church. To one family God gives ten or more children. To another family, he gives one, two, or three. And still to another he gives none. Whether we are given children or not, this is how Christians are to regard all the children in the church—as holy, precious gifts of God. Therefore, we are to raise them up in the discipline and instruction of the LORD. This requires loving them and making an investment in their lives.

The writer shrinks into one sentence a description of Boaz and Ruth's wedding ceremony and nine months of pregnancy.[3] This grammatical move takes the focus off of Boaz and Ruth and puts it on their son. We are reminded of another son given to the world by God. Obed, born in Bethlehem, was a special child. But the child born to Mary, also in Bethlehem, was *divine*. Though every child is a personal gift from God, made through a man and a woman coming together, *this* child was conceived apart from the involvement of a man. This child was born to a virgin. The Holy Spirit overshadowed Mary and a son began to grown in her womb, a child that was both human and divine in one person. This was a son conceived by the Holy Spirit and born in Bethlehem that he might die at Golgotha. As we saw in the previous chapter, the incredible birth of Obed to Boaz and Ruth points us to the miracle of the Son of God born to Mary, the child who is both David's son and David's Lord (Matt 1:18–25).

We have already stated that one of the lessons we learn from this book is that God brings life through death. He raises the dead. In the death of Elimelech and his two sons, Elimelech's name died. But with the arrival of this son, born to Ruth and Boaz, Elimelech's name and inheritance are brought back from the dead. This particular family line, from the tribe of Judah, is raised from the dead. The other son, born to Mary, was born to die but he did not stay dead. God raised his Son Jesus Christ from the dead. And with him God will raise *us* from the dead. As we go through the darkness of this age, we should remember this: God raises the dead.

A baby boy has been born in Bethlehem. Like any other community of God's people, a baby is born and the women are excited. They have something to say about this boy.

3. Block, *Judges, Ruth*, 725.

Chapter 5: Song of the Son

RUTH 4:14-15

Then the women said to Naomi, "Blessed be the LORD, who has not left you this day without a redeemer, and may his name be renowned in Israel! He shall be to you a restorer of life and a nourisher of your old age, for your daughter-in-law who loves you, who is more to you than seven sons, has given birth to him."

IN RESPONSE TO THE arrival of Boaz and Ruth's son, the women in Bethlehem burst out in praise. They are praying to God and praising his name. These words form, then, a kind of Spirit-inspired song to God; namely, a song regarding a child that has come into the world.[1]

The gathering of the women in this town happened once before in this story. In chapter 1, Naomi had returned to Bethlehem after having lived for ten years in Moab. She was joined by Ruth in her return. The women in the town see her and they collectively ask this question, "Is this Naomi?" (1:19). Naomi, apparently, had changed. It may have been that Naomi looked like death itself when she returned. Thus, her physical appearance prompted this question from the ladies in the town. *Death*, after all, is what Naomi experienced during her time in Moab. She had endured three successive deaths in Moab: the passing of her husband and her two sons. Naomi had also experienced living in a pagan nation for ten years. Moab was a godless place, and godless places are certainly able to affect a person over time,

---

1. Block writes, "The second episode of the final scene involves the women of Bethlehem, who, as in 1:19, function as a chorus in the drama." *Judges, Ruth*, 726.

not to mention the normal wear of aging ten years. So, Naomi may have shown *physical* evidence of change. We are not told this exactly. But taken all together, it is not surprising that this was the reaction of the women in the town. Something about Naomi prompted the women to wonder how this could possibly be the same Naomi that had left ten years prior.

And yet, since that moment of returning to Bethlehem, the LORD had slowly breathed life back into Naomi. This is what has been seen in her life throughout the course of this book. And God did this work in his servant Naomi primarily *through* Boaz. It was through Boaz that Naomi began to have hope, true hope for her future and the future of her family. Here we see that God had given her *life* all the more. God had already given her life through the introduction of Boaz and even earlier through Ruth's industriousness and life-long partnership (though, initially, she virtually ignored the blessing that Ruth was to her). Now she has a grandson. God continued to instill life into her and he did so here through this son.

This is what the women speak about here, the restoration of life to Naomi: "He shall be to you a restorer of life" (4:15). God was giving Naomi *life* through this grandson. This is what children are, especially in the church. Children are a picture of new life. They are *literally* new life. As they grow and as we watch them grow, we are blessed to see just this, the restoration of life. We see the restoration of generations of families. We see the bloodline continue. Children are a living picture of the way in which God brings life into the world. God is the author of life who brings things into existence that did not exist before.

This is why a baby boy or a baby girl being born in the church brings us such joy. This is what is happening among the community of God's people in Bethlehem at this time. The women are excited and they are singing because a son has been born to them. Children give us a picture of life—indeed, resurrection life. This is how we can think about the children that God gives to us. Natural birth actually does teach us something about *spiritual* birth. When we believe in Christ, Scripture describes this as being born again. This phrase is used to draw us into thinking about natural birth and what happens when a person comes to faith in Christ. He or she is *born again*. A new life is instilled in us when we believe, so much so that the Bible is not shy to refer to this change as a *birth* (John 3:1–8). Thus, children coming into the world present us with a living parable of resurrection life.

When a baby is born, pretty much everyone is excited. But who is *most* excited? It is usually the women in the community who are the most excited

Chapter 5: Song of the Son

about a new baby boy or girl. Such was the case in Bethlehem. The women joyfully praise God for the arrival of this new baby boy. In this song, we notice that the women sing primarily *to* Naomi. They are speaking *about* God, surely praising him, and they sing *about* other things, but Naomi is clearly the primary object of this song. And so, this dialogue is a decidedly feminine experience. A group of women speak to the blessings that have come upon another woman in the community. Ruth has given birth to a son, and her sisters in the town give a blessing.

This is appropriate because in God's wisdom only women bear children. The delight that this child brings is presented here through women. The next scene has Naomi holding the baby in her lap, which is another naturally feminine activity. It is appropriate then for women to be the focus in what is happening at this point in the story: "For woman was made from man, so man is now born of woman. And all things are from God" (1 Cor 11:12). Even Jesus Christ, our Savior, was born of a woman. Men have roles in raising up children in the Lord, to be sure. Raising children is not *just* a feminine activity. Where the two are available, both husband and wife are required to participate in the discipling and raising up of children in the Lord. But in God's infinite wisdom he has given the particular assignment of *bearing* children to women. This wisdom is seen in that, generally speaking, female dispositions, characteristics, and strengths are designed for just this—bearing children and caring for them. Indeed, Paul tells Timothy that in a sin-cursed world the woman would be *saved* through child bearing (1 Tim 2:15). Sometimes, the Lord does not give a particular woman children of her own. But the church is given children, and the childless woman's heart is still predisposed toward helping to care for them. Thus, a very feminine scene is depicted in these verses that revolve around a newborn boy.

With Paul's words in 1 Timothy in mind, we are able to say here that God has *saved* Naomi and he has *saved* Ruth through this child. He is a restorer of life to them. Just as God has assigned child bearing to women, he has given a special task to man in regard to his responsibilities in a family. And what is the role of the man? His role is to *redeem*. This is the role that has been given to Boaz and this is the responsibility Jesus Christ takes up as our Savior. He *redeems*. Jesus lays down his life for us and in this way, he *redeems* us.

We have already seen that the sole responsibility of redemption was laid at the feet of Boaz. He responded appropriately and became Naomi and Ruth's gō'ēl. In this song of praise though, a shift in focus happens. The women speak to Naomi, but they are praising God. And as they praise God in their address to Naomi, they sing not of Boaz, but of the son. They sing: "Blessed be the LORD, who has not left you this day without a redeemer" (Ruth 4:14). What day are they speaking of? They are speaking of the day Ruth's child was born. Thus, the title *redeemer* in their song refers to the child.

We would do well to remember here that the LORD had emptied Naomi of a husband and sons. They all died in Moab. There were no strong men in her life. Really, there were no men at all except for the men in the broader community. But God is filling her again. He is filling up that void.[2] He has given her Boaz and now he has given her a son. Again, we have seen that the LORD had appointed Boaz as a redeemer for this family. But, as was stated above, the song emphasizes the son: "He shall be to you a restorer of life and a nourisher of your old age, for your daughter-in-law who loves you, who is more to you than seven sons, has given birth to him" (v. 15). Certainly Boaz had redeemed and would continue to redeem but *the song is about the baby Obed*.[3] The redeemer for Naomi is now the son born to Ruth. Why is it this way? This is so because this son represents the revival of the name of the dead, Elimelech, and Naomi's family line. The name that came from the tribe of Judah, on the verge of extinction, has now been brought back to life. So, they sing about the son. As wonderful as Boaz's marriage to Ruth is, the women would not have been able to sing this song had the son not been born.

This is what we see in this song. This is what Boaz had mentioned over and over again at the gate in regard to redemption. Speaking to the other nameless redeemer, Boaz says, "The day you buy the field from the hand of Naomi, you also acquire Ruth the Moabite, the widow of the dead, in order to perpetuate the name of the dead in his inheritance" (v. 5). He was talking about sons. Then he speaks to the witnesses at the gate and says, "Also Ruth the Moabite, the widow of Mahlon, I have bought to be my wife, to perpetuate the name of the dead in his inheritance, that the name of the dead may not be cut off from among his brothers and from the gate of his native place" (v. 10). This son fulfills these words. The birth of this son shows that

---

2. Hubbard writes, "Yahweh's action was something he did *not* do . . . heading off the tragedy of bitter old age and familial annihilation that looms so large in the book." *Book of Ruth*, 270.

3. Block, *Judges, Ruth*, 727; Hubbard, *Book of Ruth*, 271.

Chapter 5: Song of the Son

the name of the dead has not been cut off. This family has been reborn, as it were, with the arrival of this son.

Next, the women sing about what the child will grow up to be: "He shall be to you a restorer of life and a nourisher of your old age" (v. 15). The singers are looking toward the future, as the child grows and as Naomi grows. They are thinking about the present but they are also looking toward the future. As the son and the grandmother grow together, the child will continue to give her life. This is experienced among family members with grandchildren. The children bring life to the family, in a natural sense, certainly, but in a spiritual sense as well. In healthy relationships, parents invest in their children early on, nourishing them and providing for them. Then, as the parents grow older, the children reciprocate that love by providing for their aging parents, nourishing them and supporting them. Using the words of this book, the children restore life to their parents and grandparents. Of course, something more is being said here, but they are at least referring to the natural care and love this child, once grown, will give to Naomi.

The women speak about the son and his role in the family as he grows. And they also speak about Ruth and of her relationship to Naomi: "For your daughter-in-law who loves you, who is more to you than seven sons, has given birth to him." This is how Naomi *should* regard Ruth. As was stated above, Naomi virtually disregarded Ruth's commitment to her in the beginning. But now the women sing and teach Naomi just how precious, how valuable, this daughter-in-law is to her. She is better than seven sons.[4] Seven is the number of fullness or perfection in the Bible. Naomi had been emptied of sons and now that Ruth had given birth to a son, Naomi is full. The filling up of Naomi has reached its completion.

Where once Naomi had no sons, she now has Ruth, who is better to her than seven sons, because Ruth has given her a son, a grandson. We note here that Naomi is silent. She had much to say in her bitterness. Now she can only be still, beholding the goodness of God in the face of this boy, and listening to the voices of the women praising God that he has made Naomi whole again.

The women also describe Ruth as the "daughter-in-law who loves you." Here *love* is not primarily defined by Ruth's feelings toward Naomi. This is not how the writer has presented Ruth's love for Naomi throughout

---

4. Hubbard writes, "To say that one woman was worth seven men was the ultimate tribute—particularly in a story absorbed with having a son!" *Book of Ruth*, 273–74.

this book. Rather, Ruth's love for Naomi has been demonstrated by what Ruth has *done* for Naomi.[5] And this is where true love is found, in covenant obedience, self-denying *action* for the sake of another. Does Ruth love Naomi? Yes, she had proven her love by her actions earlier in the story. She left her homeland to follow Naomi into a country foreign to her own, to a foreign people, and to a God very much unlike the gods she knew in Moab. She had given up her former life for Naomi and now she has given up her very *body* by carrying this son and giving birth to him. Why did she do this? Because she *loved* Naomi. Our love for God is shown by our actions. Our love for neighbor is shown by our actions. Our words are taken into account in regard to how we love, this much is true. We are to be gracious to one another with our words. We use words to express our feelings. But the words only have meaning if they are backed up by *deeds*.

The women speak highly of Ruth, but the words about Ruth draw us past Ruth to the son: "For your daughter-in-law who loves you, who is more to you than seven sons, has given birth to him." This song is directed to Naomi. It mentions Ruth, but it is really about the son. We are reminded of the birth of our Lord Jesus Christ to Mary. When Jesus was born, his arrival caused angels to sing (Luke 2:13–14). Mary, Christ's mother, sang when she knew that Jesus was growing in her womb (Luke 1:46–55). Simeon responded to the birth of Christ with a song (Luke 2:28–32). And what was the content of these songs when they see the child and hear about him? They essentially say, "A Redeemer has been born and he will be to Israel and to all who believe in him a restorer of life." He is One who can give his people life, *eternal* life. This is why they sing. And this is why this grandchild is so important. This is why these women sing in response to Obed's arrival. God was preparing the way for Christ to come. He is the supreme restorer of life and the true Redeemer. He is the greater Obed and the greater David. This is why it was appropriate that this song was sung and that the words were written down for our instruction. The arrival of this son points us to the arrival of our Savior, Jesus Christ, in history.

Christians do this every week. We respond with praise to God that Christ has come. He came to this world, he died, and he was raised from the dead. He returned to the Father and thus is no longer physically with us today, but he is coming again. This is why we sing. We sing because God has not left us in the dark. He did not leave Naomi in the dark. He did not abandon her to her widowhood. He *saved* her. He gave her a redeemer through

---

5. Block, *Judges, Ruth*, 729.

Chapter 5: Song of the Son

this son. And in so doing, God foreshadowed the sending of his own Son, our Savior and Restorer of life, into our world through Mary.

The women speak of Naomi's old age in this song. Her old age can be seen as representing long-lasting life that would be nourished through the strength this son would provide. Thus, it is resurrection life that is painted all over these verses. It is the resurrection life that our Lord gives us now and forevermore. Jesus said, "Everyone who lives and believes in me shall never die" (John 11:26). The Lord would see to it that Naomi would never die: "He shall be to you a restorer of life." And he would ultimately do this through his own Son.

We see that God was preparing the way for this Son. Jesus had not yet come when these events took place. But Obed is here now. He is the grandfather of David. This is the lineage of Jesus Christ. God was working. With the arrival of Ruth's son, Naomi and all of Israel had been given new life, a shot in the arm to restore their strength. The boy would need a name. We will consider the significance of the name in the next chapter.

Chapter 6: Servant

RUTH 4:16-17

Then Naomi took the child and laid him on her lap and became his nurse. And the women of the neighborhood gave him a name, saying, "A son has been born to Naomi." They named him Obed. He was the father of Jesse, the father of David.

THE SCENE AT THE end of this story is entirely domestic. It is ordinary, mundane. Naomi is holding her grandson in her lap. What significance is there for God's people and for the world in talking about a grandmother and her grandson?

We are told that Naomi held the baby born to Boaz and Ruth in her lap and that she became the boy's nurse. This indicates that Naomi would be intimately involved in the care of the child.[1] Naomi would help nourish him and protect him. Already, the intimacy of this work is portrayed. Naomi is holding the boy in her lap. She is touching him. She is embracing him. Being a nurse requires this kind of physical interaction. Thus, the scene is rather ordinary.

Many Christians know what it is like to hold a grandchild in their lap and experience the sense of fullness this can bring. Is one's heart not full holding the children of her children in her hands? Is one not satisfied feeling a grandchild pressed against her chest? This is what has happened with Naomi. At the beginning of the story Naomi had been emptied. The picture we had of her then was of an elderly widow ravaged by death and emptied

---

1. Block, *Judges, Ruth*, 730.

Chapter 6: Servant

of life and future.[2] Her physical appearance may have been significantly altered. This may have been what prompted the women of Bethlehem to ask the question "Is this Naomi?" upon seeing her for the first time in ten years since she left the city to take up residence in Moab. At that time, she was barren, devoid of a husband and sons. She had been emptied of life and was *full* of bitterness.

But God had filled her again. He had given her life upon life: a new son-in-law in Boaz, the daughter-in-law Ruth, and now Ruth's son. Notice how Naomi does not speak here. In fact, the last words that we heard from Naomi are found back in chapter 3. The day after Ruth met with Boaz at the threshing floor Naomi said this to Ruth: "Wait, my daughter, until you learn how the matter turns out, for the man will not rest but will settle the matter today" (3:18). We now fast forward at least ten months from that day. Naomi is holding her grandson and we still do not have any recorded words from Naomi.

When she first arrived in Bethlehem, she had much to say. She was bitter and she gladly *voiced* her bitterness. Now she is silent. What has happened? God has spoken. By his word, the men in Naomi's life were taken away. And now, by his word, he fills Naomi with this grandson. In the face of such abundant grace and mercy Naomi is speechless.

But there are others who speak in her place. The other women speak about the boy and about Naomi, saying simply, "A son has been born to Naomi." We may return to our discussion about the ordinary character of this scene. There is nothing spectacular about this ending. Naomi is holding her grandson. But if we set it against what had happened to Naomi we may be able to more fully appreciate the power in its simplicity and peacefulness.

Naomi had known famine and death, sojourning in a foreign land. In a word, she had known *chaos*. Because of God's mercy, all of that was behind her now. In addition to this, the writer sets this scene against the future as well. We are told that the women of the neighborhood name the child saying, "A son has been born to Naomi" (4:17).[3] The women here, alongside Naomi, represent, in a way, *all* of Israel. The naming of the child by the Israelite women and their statement that a son had been born to

---

2. Block writes, "She had not only had her bread basket emptied by famine; in the deaths of her husband and sons her bosom had also been emptied of men." *Judges, Ruth*, 730.

3. On the uniqueness of the child being named by someone other than the parents see Hubbard, *Book of Ruth*, 276, and Block, *Judges, Ruth*, 731.

Naomi (even though, technically, he was born to Ruth) signified that this son belongs to *Israel*. This is *Israel's* son. A similar declaration is seen in Isaiah: "For to us a child is born, to us a son is given" (Isa 9:6).

In the New Testament, when the shepherds in the field saw an angel of the Lord, who was there to announce the birth of Mary's son, Jesus, the angel said to them, "I bring you good news of great joy that will be for all the people. For unto you is born this day in the city of David a Savior, who is Christ the Lord" (Luke 2:10–11). This child was born to *Mary*, but the angel essentially says to the Israelite shepherds, "This is your son." This was appropriate because this is who Jesus Christ was and is—the promised Son born to Israel. He was the son of Israel who would bring "great joy . . . for all the people." So, this child Naomi holds, in a significant way, is Israel's son. Thus, the Bethlehemite *community*, in supporting the parents, were obligated to help this family in its care of him and they were to continually pray for him.

What is significant about this son? As we have stated, the writer takes us into the future. This *son* will have a child as well. He would, presumably, marry a woman and have a son with her. That son would be named Jesse. Jesse would also marry and *his* wife would give birth to a son. In fact, we learn that Jesse's wife gave birth to *eight* sons! (1 Sam 16:10–11). The youngest was named David. And that son, David, Naomi's great-great-grandson, became the king of Israel. In God's infinite wisdom, he chose the weak and the lowly to shame the strong (1 Cor 1:26–29).

In this story we have now seen God use the domestic and ordinary to advance his kingdom and bring glory to his name: a grandmother holding her grandson and becoming his nurse, the humility and faithfulness of a son, Boaz, and the quiet trust and courage of a daughter, Ruth. God used all of this to save his people.

This is a good lesson for individuals and families in the church. We would do well to appreciate the ordinary, the domestic. Churches may often seem to only care about what the world cares about—fame, praise of men, money, and worldly success or influence. Ruth teaches us that what pleases God is quiet faithfulness. We are taught here to always have a healthy concern for how our present activity will serve future generations. We are not talking about training the future generation just to be polite, stable members of society, though this is certainly good. We are talking about training future generations to be faithful *Christians* in a broken age. The book of Ruth encourages the church to aim for quiet faithfulness to God's word.

Chapter 6: Servant

We are told here that the women of Bethlehem name the son. This action by the women of Judah is not seen anywhere else in the Old Testament. We do see a similar scene, however, in the New Testament. When John the Baptist was born, we are told that the neighbors and the relatives rejoiced with Elizabeth (Luke 1:57–58). We learn also that the community might have been involved in the naming of the child: "And they would have called him Zechariah after his father, but his mother answered 'No; he shall be called John'" (vv. 59–60). The community, apparently, thought that he should have been called Zechariah after his father. However, both his mother, Elizabeth, and his father, Zechariah, were obedient to the angel from heaven and thus named him John (Luke 1:8–13; 59–63).[4] So, it is not likely that Boaz and Ruth had no part at all in naming their son. But what is clear is that this community of women rejoiced with Naomi and Ruth that a son had been born and that son was given the name Obed.

Two times we are told that the women named the child: "And the women of the neighborhood gave him a name.... They named him Obed" (Ruth 4:17). The meaning of this name would have been known to just about any Jewish person at this time. The name means *servant*.[5] Obadiah means *servant of the* LORD. Thus, the child is named servant. What a fitting name! A servant has been born to two servants. Is this not what has been seen in Boaz and Ruth all along—servanthood? They were true servants, serving one another, serving the community, and serving God's glory. So, it only makes sense that their son is called *servant*.

And it also makes sense that the servant's grandson David became king. A true and good king is a servant. That is what David was. He was serving in the fields as a shepherd when God called him. David served Israel's first king, Saul, for a time, playing music for him on the lyre. David served on the battlefield as a young man contending against Goliath and gaining victory over him. At that time, David was speaking to Saul about Goliath, convincing Saul to let him onto the battlefield with the giant. In that speech to King Saul, David referred to himself as *your servant* three times (1 Sam 17:32–37).

After suffering much by the hand of Saul, David was finally made king. What did he do as king? He *served*. He was a servant to Israel all the

---

4. Hubbard writes, "Luke 1:59 apparently presupposes a custom whereby friends and relatives named newborn infants, and a similar ancient (local?) custom may underlie this naming." *Book of Ruth*, 276.

5. Hubbard, *Book of Ruth*, 276–77. See also Holladay, *Concise*, 262.

days he reigned. To be sure, he was not perfect. But overall, his time on the throne was marked by service. So, when Jesus comes, the *King of kings*, the son of David, and David's Lord, what does Jesus have to say about his own reign as king? "The Son of Man came not to be served but to serve, and to give his life as a ransom for many" (Matt 20:28). Jesus came to be an Obed, a servant.

In Ruth, emphasis is laid upon the domestic and the ordinary. There are a grandmother and her grandson. We have seen a husband and wife come together and have a baby. A small community rejoices together with this family that a son had been born in Israel. He was to be called servant. Similar themes are found at the crucifixion of Christ. The cross is actually *less* than ordinary—it is humiliating and shameful. He was one cursed by God.

And yet, at the same time, this ordinary scene in Ruth forms a prelude to a king being born in Israel: "They named him Obed. He was the father of Jesse, the father of David" (Ruth 4:17). Similarly for Christ, the humiliation of the cross and the darkness of the grave gave way to the glory of his powerful resurrection on the third day and the light of the gospel going to all nations.

There is a lesson here for all Christians about what it means to be a follower of Christ in this world. First and foremost, we are to be *servants*. We are to be servants to one another and servants to the Lord. We are to be servants especially to the weakest ones among us. Leadership in the church and in Christian families should be marked by this—servanthood. In order to properly be first in the church, one must make himself *last*. He must be a servant to all, like Boaz and Ruth, like David, like Christ.

Finally, in our service to one another, we would do well to have a greater appreciation for the domestic and ordinary, the mundane. Let us embrace doing the secret, hidden things. Let us joyfully perform those acts of service that are never seen. As a Christian, washing dishes, taking out the trash, going to work every day, practicing piano, practicing a particular sport, attending school, going on dates, creating shopping lists, eating dinner together, attending worship services, attending Sunday school, teaching Sunday school, and all the other countless activities that may seem rather ordinary in the eyes of the world should all be seen in a new light—the light of Scripture. We are serving a king. Our service and obedience, our self-sacrifice and striving after holiness in the *domestic* realm are pleasing to our Father and to our King in the *divine* realm. It is not ultimately about

Chapter 6: Servant

us—it is about God's glory and the glory of our King, Jesus. Our goal and our hope for the church should be taken from what we see here. These are servants raising other servants who also raise up other servants in God's kingdom. In a word, we should be after generational faithfulness to God: "They named him Obed. He was the father of Jesse, the father of David" (v. 17).

Although we must review our writer's epilogue in the next chapter, we have reached the end of the book. And we have arrived at a glorious conclusion to Naomi's personal history. Obed has been born. His grandson would be king. What a wonderful ending to a story that began with so much tragedy. This was God's plan from all eternity, played out before our eyes in the history of this family and in the history of the Israelite people "in the days when the judges ruled" (1:1).

Chapter 7: Breach

RUTH 4:18-22

Now these are the generations of Perez: Perez fathered Hezron, Hezron fathered Ram, Ram fathered Amminadab, Amminadab fathered Nahshon, Nahshon fathered Salmon, Salmon fathered Boaz, Boaz fathered Obed, Obed fathered Jesse, and Jesse fathered David.

THESE FINAL VERSES OF Ruth comprise a genealogy. And the genealogy forms a kind of epilogue to the story.[1] This epilogue ends with the name David. The last image we get in this story is of Naomi holding an infant boy, David's grandfather, in her lap. Thus, we learn from this genealogy that the book of Ruth is really about the ascension of David and how Boaz and Ruth, and Naomi as well, fit into David's history. The final word is not famine nor widowhood nor the end of bloodlines. The final word is *David*.[2]

This section begins, "Now these are the generations of Perez . . . " Genealogies were a typical part of Jewish writings. They were not given simply to supply a formal record of names, though they do serve this purpose. Genealogies send messages. One message this particular genealogy delivers is that David had the right to sit on the throne of Israel. He is the promised prince from the tribe of Judah. Perez was a son of Judah. In Genesis, Jacob prophesied that a royal figure would be born from this

---

1. Block, *Judges, Ruth*, 733. Block refers to it as a genealogical epilogue.

2. Hubbard writes, "As the book's concluding word, however, *David*, sounded the triumph of God's providence over the vicissitudes suffered by the names listed." *Book of Ruth*, 285.

Chapter 7: Breach

line, Judah's line. Though this lineage included a Moabite woman, Ruth, and the less-than-honorable circumstances of Judah and Tamar having a child (Perez) together, this genealogy was part of the official record of King David's bloodline.

Numbers were often used in Jewish writings to signify something. Specific numbers, like genealogies, sent messages. They often represented a deeper truth. For example, the number seven is used to represent perfection or completion. One might think of the seven days of creation in the beginning when the heavens and the earth were completed. Certainly the creation account refers to days in history, but that there were specifically *seven* days forms the backdrop for the way the number seven is used elsewhere. We have seen an example of the symbolic use of numbers in this book when the women of Bethlehem praise God for blessing Naomi with a grandson through Ruth: "He shall be to you a restorer of life and a nourisher of your old age, for your daughter-in-law who loves you, who is more to you than seven sons, has given birth to him" (v. 15). As was stated earlier in chapter 5 on page 115, the number seven here represents perfection or fullness. Ruth is better to Naomi than the life-giving fullness that would come along with having not just five or six sons but *seven* sons.

The number ten also symbolizes fullness in the Old Testament. We may think of the ten commandments given at Mt. Sinai or the ten plagues that came upon Egypt. Daniel saw a vision of four beasts, each symbolizing various earthly kings and the power of their respective kingdoms. The last beast was described as terrifying and exceedingly strong. This last beast had ten horns signifying the fullness or completion of its power in comparison to the others (Dan 7:1–22). The New Testament picks up this symbolic use of numbers as well. Matthew arranged his genealogy of Christ into three evenly distributed generations: "So all the generations from Abraham to David were fourteen generations, and from David to the deportation to Babylon fourteen generations, and from the deportation to Babylon to the Christ fourteen generations" (Matt 1:17). The genealogy sends a message—Jesus is the rightful heir to the throne of David. Additionally, this arrangement of three sets of fourteen symbolizes the perfection of divine wisdom seen throughout Israel's history as Yahweh was preparing the way for the coming of Christ.

With all of this in mind, we see here that the writer has arranged this genealogy into ten generations. It could be that something similar to what we see at the beginning of Matthew is being done here. A message is sent.

Part IV: Redemption and Royalty

Though the personal histories behind some of the names listed appear to the human eye as mere randomness and virtual chaos, the story of Ruth reminds us to look again with eyes of faith. The perfection of God's wisdom and the fullness of his power rules out over the sins, failures, and disappointments of his people.

This may explain why the writer begins with Perez. Why is Judah not listed first? Judah, after all, was one of the twelve patriarchs of Israel. We mentioned already in this work that Jacob prophesied about Judah's future children. A royal figure would come from his line.[3] This son of Judah would rule the nations. If the writer wanted to prove the legitimacy of David's kingship it would seem reasonable to begin the genealogy of David with Judah. However, if this was done, we would have eleven generations listed and not ten.

In our day, we may not appreciate the significance of numbers like the Jewish writers did (although we should appreciate their significance in certain parts of Scripture). But if we stop to think about it, we, at times, do value the symbolic meaning of certain numbers. We might think about the passwords we use for our accounts, computers, or phones. Do we normally choose random numbers? Generally, we don't. We often pick numbers that spell out a name based on the letters associated with each on a phone. We will choose the numbers of the date of a birthday or anniversary. The writer here has arranged this genealogy into ten generations, perhaps to emphasize the perfection of God's will in tying these lives together. This would include the life of a Moabite woman, at one point widowed and living as a poor stranger in Israel, and the life of an Israelite land owner, Boaz, at one point a stranger to Ruth and Naomi and ignorant of the dire circumstances surrounding his kinsmen's family.

There may be something else, though. One element in all of this that we may consider is that Boaz has taken the place of Mahlon in this line. Because of the grace of God and because of his self-sacrifice and faithfulness Boaz's name is remembered forever. But what of Perez? And what of Perez's connection to David?

Perez was a twin. He was born to Judah and Tamar amidst circumstances that to the human eye would seem unlikely to produce ancestors of a worthy man like Boaz and a king like David.[4] We saw in a previous chapter that Tamar was the daughter-in-law of Judah, but her husband,

---

3. Gen 49:8–13.
4. Gen 38:1–30.

Chapter 7: Breach

Judah's son, had died. Seeing that Judah was not acting upon his promise to give her another son to be her husband, Tamar disguised herself and drew Judah in to producing an heir with her. She conceived and gave birth to twins. Perez was one of these twins. When the time had come for Tamar to give birth, Perez's brother, Zerah, stuck out his hand. The midwife tied a scarlet thread around his hand to signify that he came out first. The thread identified him as the firstborn son who would receive all the rights and benefits that come along with this distinction.

But as Zerah drew back his hand, Perez came out *before* his brother! When the midwife saw this happen, she said, "What a breach you have made for yourself!" Thus *Perez*, not Zerah, was the firstborn son to Judah. He was aptly named Perez, which means "breach" in the Hebrew language. This meant that Perez was the unexpected one. His brother's hand came out first and was *expected* to be the firstborn son. The scarlet thread signified this expectation. Perez surprised the midwife, making a breach for himself and coming out into the world *before* his brother.

In the context of Ruth, it makes sense to begin with Perez here. He is the unexpected one, whose descendants would become leaders like the honorable prince and tribal leader of Judah, Nahshon, who is on this list alongside David. The expectation for a genealogy of the highly revered King David, of the tribe of Judah, might be that no gentiles would be listed. Surely the bloodline of *David* would be pure. And yet, behind Boaz's name is his wife, Ruth, a Moabite. And Matthew tells us that behind the name of Boaz's father, Salmon, is another gentile woman, Rahab (Matt 1:5–6).

Boaz, in a sense, made a breach for himself when he chose to redeem Ruth. David also, the eighth-born son to Jesse, was an unexpected choice for king. He was just a boy when he killed Goliath. The three oldest brothers were originally sent into battle against the Philistines. David was the youngest, a keeper of sheep, and handsome in appearance. The *expectation* would have been that one of his older, battle-tested brothers would be chosen as king. But it was not so. David broke into the history of Israel's kingdom in that he was chosen to be king though he was the youngest son of Jesse and untested in battle.

Why is David here ultimately? Why Boaz or Perez? They are included here because of God's sovereign election. God *chose* David. God *chose* Boaz. God determined that Perez would come out first. Before the foundation of the world God chose them. Yahweh *brought* Ruth to Boaz. The LORD *gave* Ruth a son. God chose Mary to be the mother of his only-begotten Son, the greater David. And in Jesus's birth he gave the world its only Savior. As John the Gospel writer tells us, "For God so loved the world that he gave his only Son" (John 3:16).

God chose Naomi, Boaz, and Ruth, and he determined to have their story written down for us so that we might see how their histories fit into the history of a *king*! Part of what this genealogy reminds us of, then, is that God has chosen *you*. If you have faith in the true Redeemer, Jesus Christ, you belong in the kingdom of God. Your home is with God's church. You have been called to serve God's glory in your family and in the church through your worship and fellowship. What this means for you is that you should not expect to become famous in the world's eyes. You should not expect to receive the praise of men or worldly influence. This is what the unbelieving world is after. What should Christians seek?

Boaz, Ruth, Naomi, and Ruth's son, Obed, at this time were quietly living and working in Bethlehem. It was not possible then for them to fully understand their significance in Israel's history, much less their place in the *world's* history. We would do well to meditate on this truth for a moment. If you are reading this and you are Christian, you are serving Christ today and worshiping him partly because of what God was doing thousands of years ago in this little unknown family in Bethlehem. Boaz and Ruth likely will never go down in the world's history books as legendary figures. But in regard to the history of his people, God made sure that part of their lives was written down. In *his* eyes, they are important. And they are now honored in every generation of the Lord's body.

These figures in redemptive history are honored by God. Despite the suffering and hardships, they responded to God's love with faithfulness, hard work, and perseverance. Their obedience was not perfect but it was pleasing in God's eyes. Boaz and Ruth could not see thousands of years into the future. They could not see how the creation and the growth of their little family was part of a plan of salvation that would touch every corner of the world. But this is what God does. He uses what is insignificant in the world's eyes to do things that are profoundly significant in his. We do not know how far reaching our faithfulness today will be. But this is the kind of life God calls us to—a life lived by faith, not by sight.

He has chosen us and called us into fellowship with his Son, Jesus Christ our Lord (1 Cor 1:9). This calling includes the obligation to live a life of self-denial, a life of daily taking up our cross and dying to ourselves, for the sake of those closest to us and for the sake of the church. Dear Christian,

Chapter 7: Breach

your name may not find a place in the history books of the world. But it is already found in another book. Before the foundation of the world your name was written down in the book of life of the Lamb who was slain (Rev 13:8). There will be setbacks, heartache, and disappointment. There may be unfaithfulness and wickedness all around. But you are in union with the resurrected Christ. Because of him you will always be remembered.

In this genealogy the writer looks back into that history of Israel's preeminent king. Among Old Testament figures (next to Moses perhaps), David holds the highest place relative to prestige and importance.[5] Moses spoke of David in the book of Deuteronomy: "When you come to the land that the LORD your God is giving you, and you possess it and dwell in it and then say, 'I will set a king over me, like all the nations that are around me,' you may indeed set a king over you whom the LORD your God will choose" (Deut 17:14–15). Much of Samuel, Kings, and Chronicles deals with the kingship of David. Even when subsequent kings appear, the writer often compares that king to David: "Josiah was eight years old when he began to reign, and he reigned thirty-one years in Jerusalem. And he did what was right in the eyes of the LORD, and walked in the ways of David his father; and he did not turn aside to the right hand or to the left" (2 Kgs 22:1–2). David wrote the majority of the Psalms. The Gospel writer Matthew begins his Gospel by legitimizing Jesus Christ as the son of David through a genealogy like this one in Ruth. Toward the end of this same Gospel, we hear the people celebrating the entrance of Jesus into Jerusalem with the exclamation: "Hosanna to the Son of David!"[6] And in the last book of the Bible, Jesus refers to himself as "the holy one, the true one, who has the key of David, who opens and no one will shut, who shuts and no one opens" (Rev 3:7).

Thus, the Spirit speaking to us in Scripture enables us to see that King David is highly honored because his kingship is but a shadow of the true King, Jesus Christ. David points us to Christ. In David, in the *righteousness* of David, we see traces of the righteousness of Christ, the true King of Israel, *our* true King. It was the righteousness of Christ, his Spirit, at work in these figures in Ruth all along. So, this genealogy at the end of this little book partly explains a profound truth. In the days when there was no king in Israel, God was secretly preparing the way for a righteous king to be born in Israel, and specifically in Bethlehem. Israel lost itself in a downward spiral

---

5. Block, *Judges, Ruth*, 735.
6. Hubbard, *Book of Ruth*, 285.

of immorality. But Ruth teaches us that in the midst of spiritual darkness the light of King David was already beginning to shine, refracting the true light—Jesus Christ—who would come into the world. This was the ultimate breach. The day heaven came down to earth. And at the cross, where this greater David was hung to die, the love of God broke into our world and saved us. It is the name, *Jesus Christ*, the son of David and the Son of God, that wins out in the end. Dear reader, receive this message.

Conclusion

AT THE TIME OF writing this conclusion, an unexplained explosion occurred in a neighborhood near my home. It was recorded on a door camera and posted online. It did not look like something domestic. Rather, the explosion was fierce, like that seen in footage of military operations. Thankfully, no one was hurt. However, residents living miles away reported that the detonation briefly shook their houses. It is the prayer of this author that, like the walls and windows of these homes, you have felt something of the inherent power of Ruth through this exposition. For Ruth is not like other written works. To be sure, it is a historical account, a story of a family that lived in real time. But it is more than this—it is the word of God. And the word speaks about itself. It attests that it is *living* and *active* (Heb 4:12). Though Ruth is part of the Old Testament and therefore written prior to the coming of the Messiah, it contains within it the redemptive power of God's message of salvation now fully revealed in that Messiah, Jesus, God's Son crucified for sinners (John 3:16; Rom 5:8). In Ruth, then, we have, in types and shadows, the very substance of this gospel (Col 2:16–17). This is why these seemingly insignificant events, involving rather ordinary people, can truly have an effect on others living thousands of years apart from them. May the Holy Spirit be pleased to shake the windows and walls of your *heart* through what you have read here. And may this lead you, like Ruth, to take refuge under the wings of the God of Israel (Ruth 2:12).

Bibliography

Block, Daniel I. *Judges, Ruth*. The New American Commentary 6. Nashville: B&H, 1999.

Ferguson, Sinclair B. *Faithful God: An Exposition of the Book of Ruth*. Wales: Bryntirion, 2013.

Holladay, William L. *A Concise Hebrew and Aramaic Lexicon of the Old Testament*. Grand Rapids: Eerdmans, 1988.

Hubbard, Robert L., Jr. *The Book of Ruth*. The New International Commentary on the Old Testament. Grand Rapids: Eerdmans, 1988.

Longman III, Tremper, and Raymond B. Dillard. *An Introduction to the Old Testament*. 2nd ed. Grand Rapids: Zondervan Academic, 2006.

Walton, John H., et al. *Old Testament*. Vol. 1 of *The Bible Background Commentary*. Downers Grove, IL: InterVarsity, 2000.

The Westminster Standard. "Larger Catechism." https://thewestminsterstandard.org/westminster-larger-catechism/.

———. "Shorter Catechism." https://thewestminsterstandard.org/westminster-shorter-catechism/.

———. "The Westminster Confession of Faith." https://thewestminsterstandard.org/the-westminster-confession/#Chapter%20XXV.

www.ingramcontent.com/pod-product-compliance
Lightning Source LLC
Chambersburg PA
CBHW072152160426
43197CB00012B/2345